# 20+ CREATIVE WAYS TO

# Decorate

# EGGS

## (for Easter or any time)

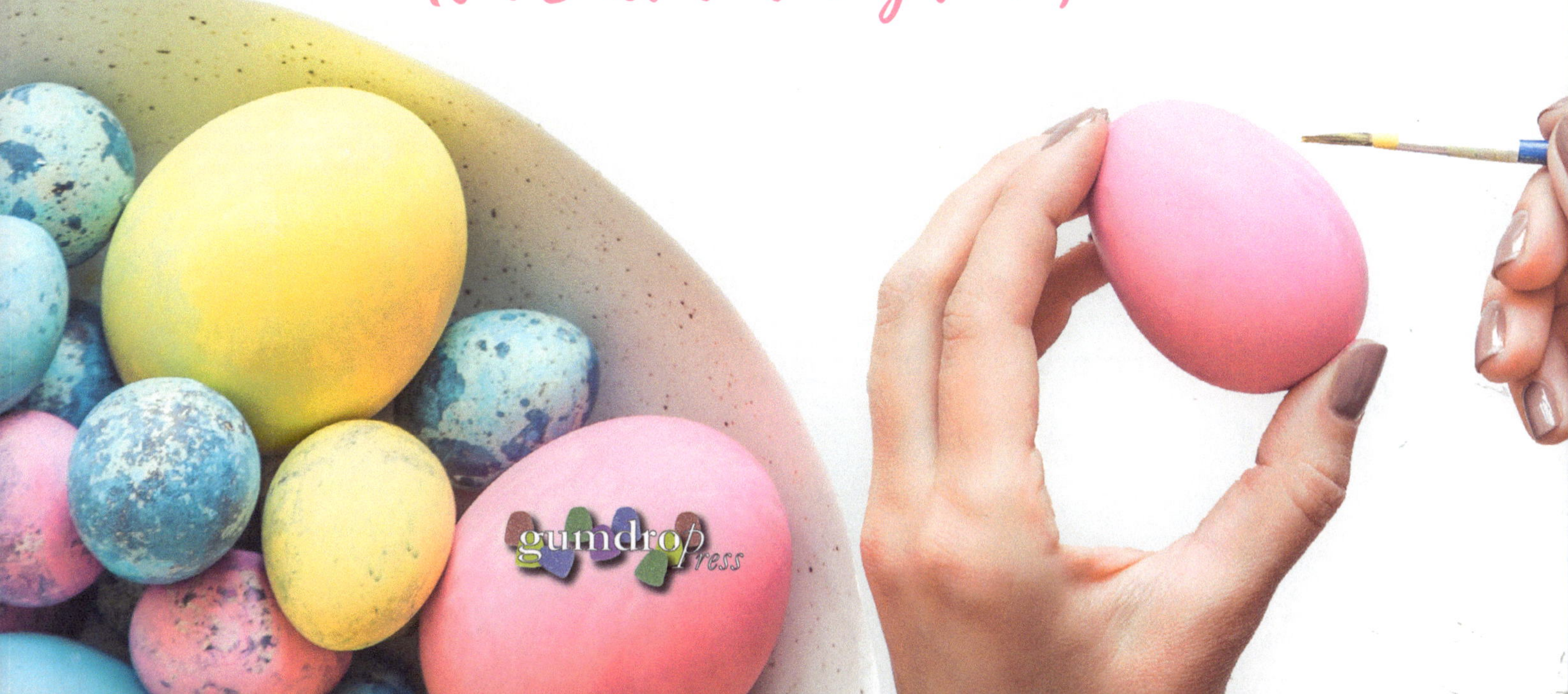

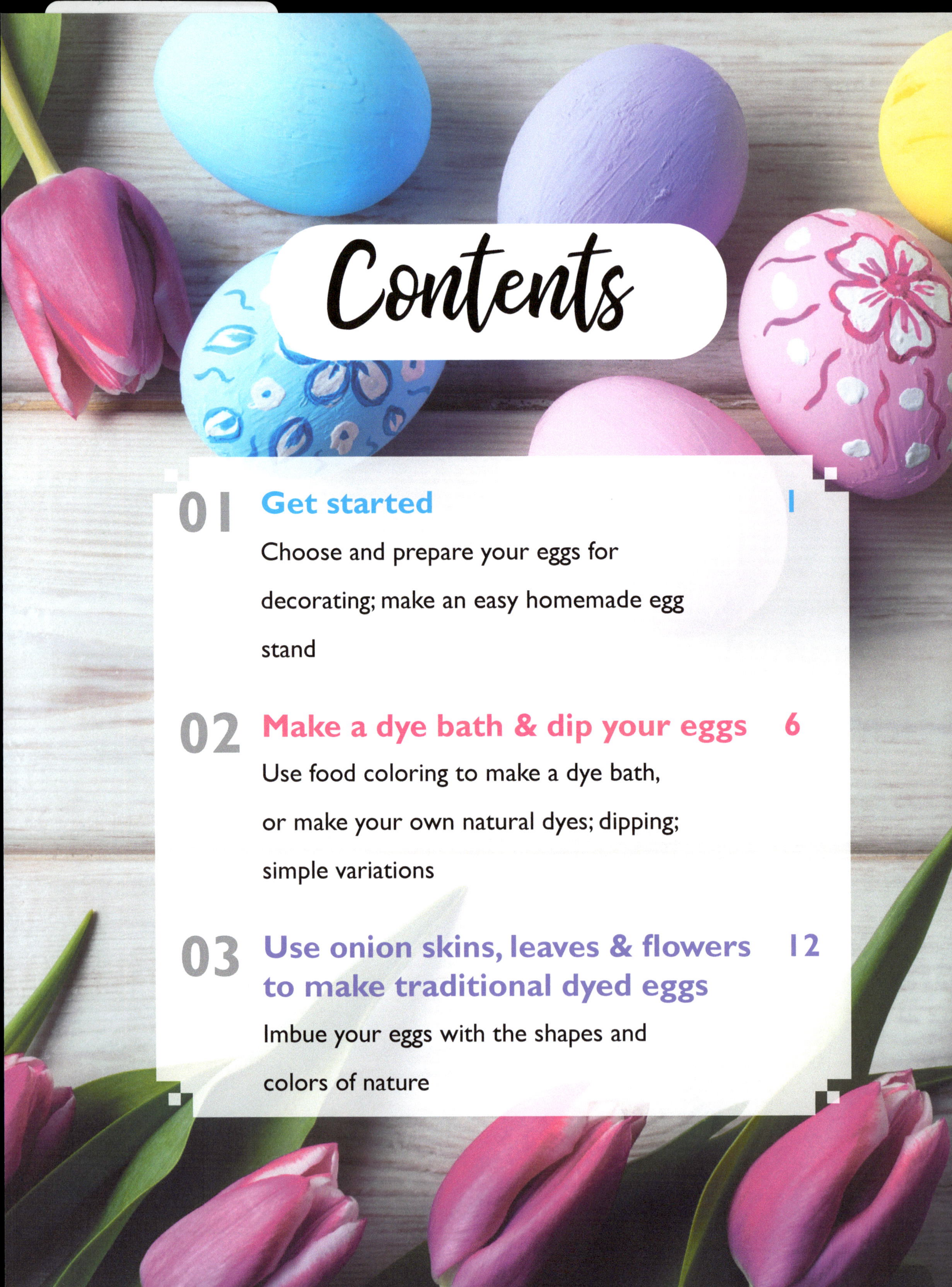

# Contents

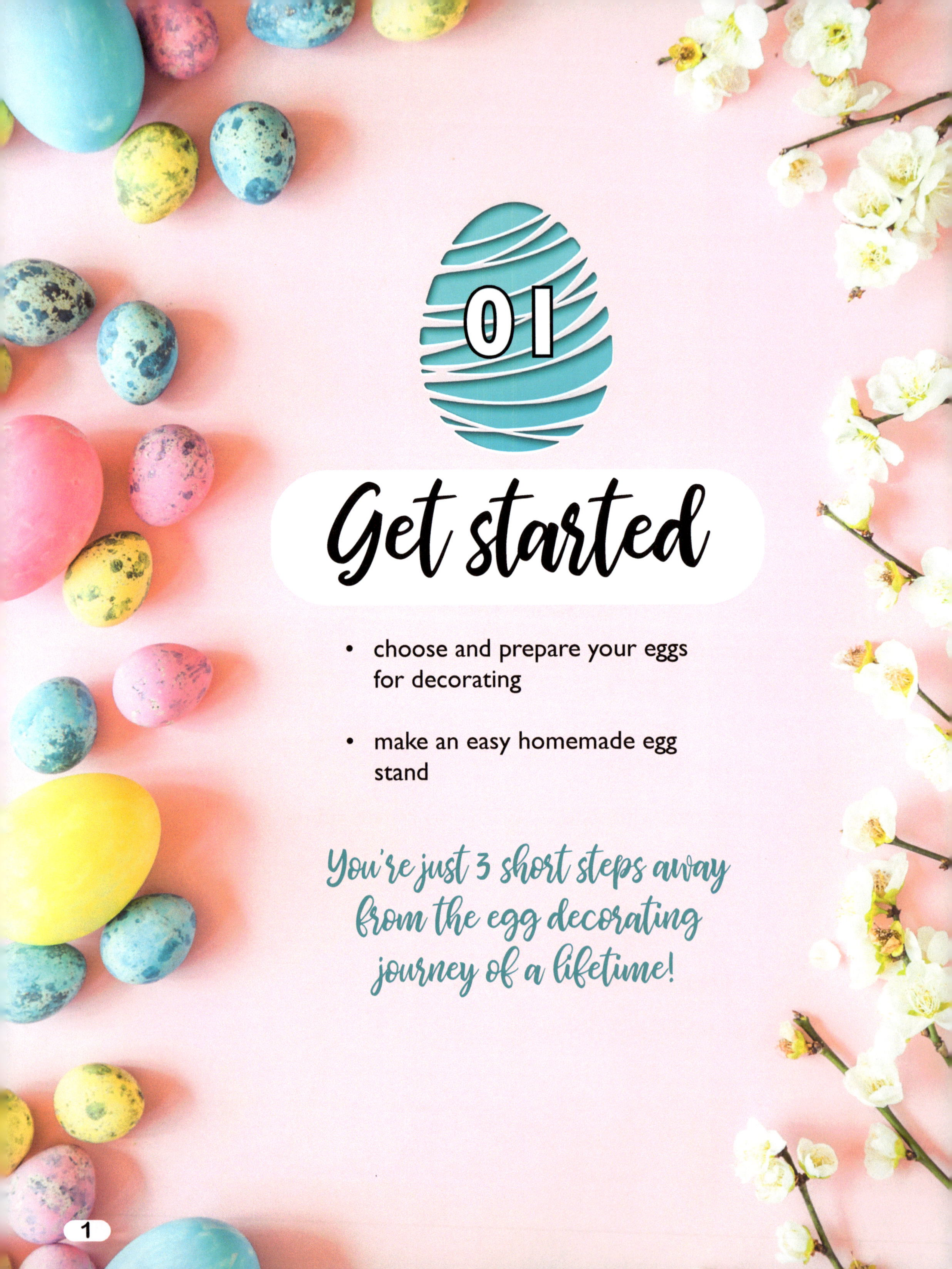

# 01

# Get started

- choose and prepare your eggs for decorating

- make an easy homemade egg stand

You're just 3 short steps away from the egg decorating journey of a lifetime!

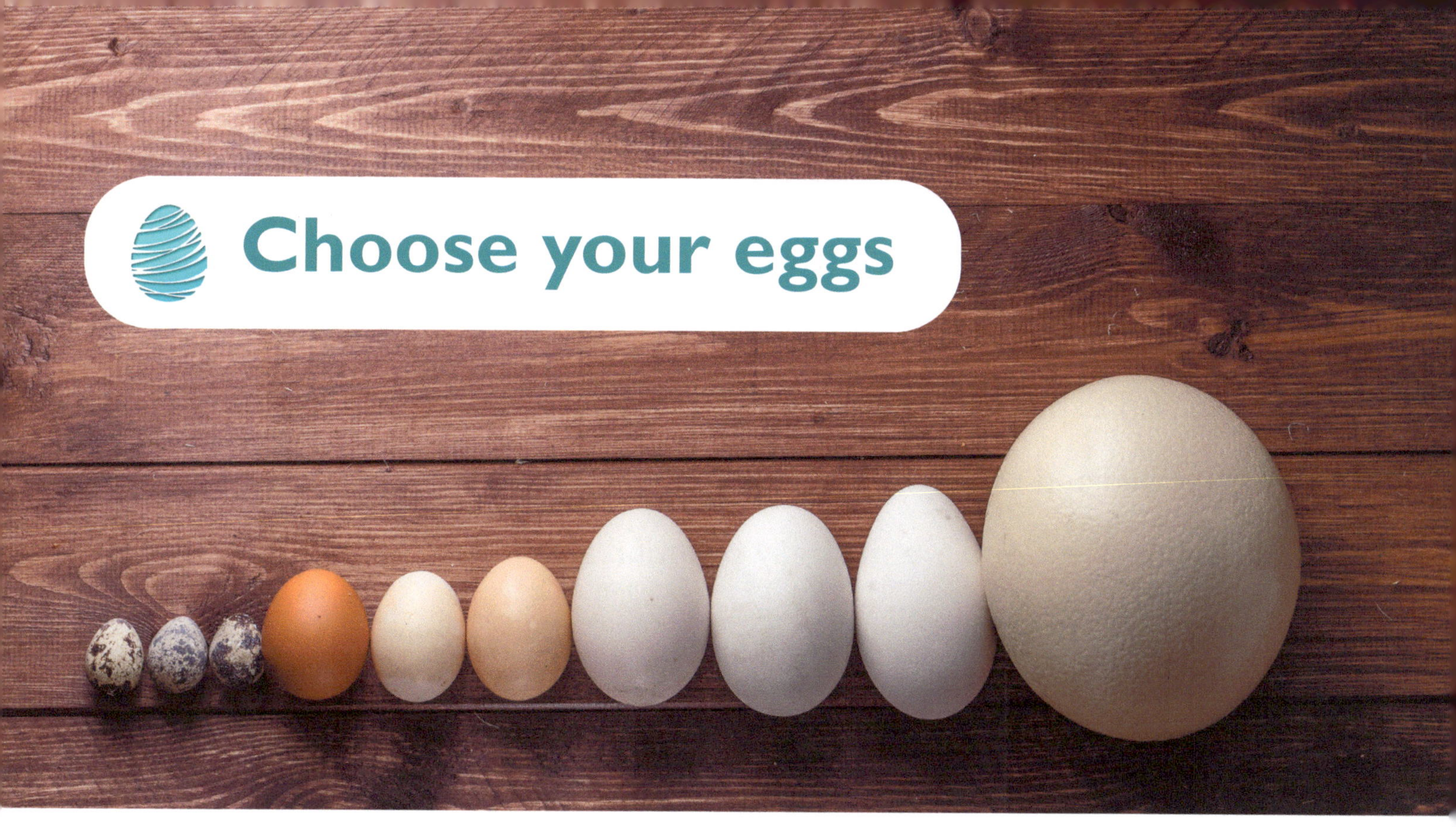

The chicken eggs we're used to seeing in cartons at the grocery store aren't the only kinds of eggs out there. Depending on where you live and shop, you might be able to find other kinds of domestic fowl eggs. Quail eggs, which are around half the size of a typical chicken egg, can be used to create a pretty garland or even a necklace. Goose eggs are about twice the size of chicken eggs, while duck eggs are about halfway between a chicken and goose egg.

Ostrich eggs are positively gigantic!

Don't forget that even the common chicken egg comes in a range of sizes. Using different sizes of eggs can add visual interest to a decorated egg display or project.

You can also experiment with using white and brown, speckled and unspeckled eggs. Never use wild bird eggs, though—those are naturally beautiful and many species are protected.

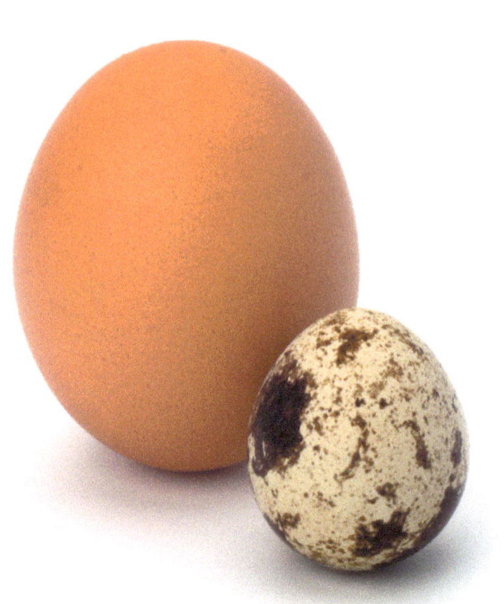

# 🥚 Prepare your eggs

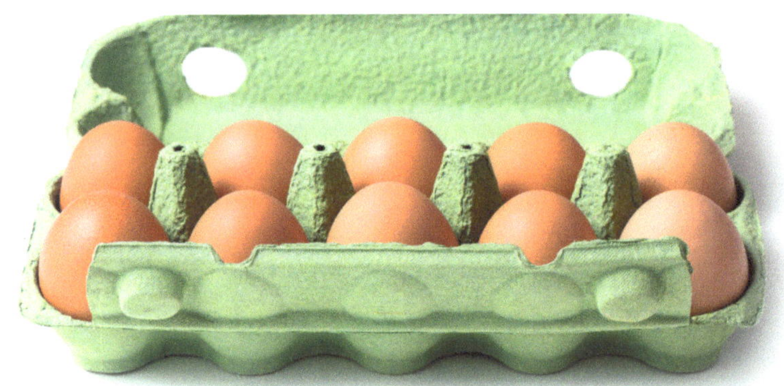

You have two basic options for preparing your eggs for decorating: you can hard boil them or blow them.

## Hard boil

Hard boil the eggs if you want to eat them later (and can bear to destroy the beautiful shells you make!). The USDA says that hard-boiled eggs are safe to eat for up to 7 days but should not be kept out of the refrigerator (unless on ice) for more than 2 hours. One of the added advantages of hard-cooking eggs is that the insides also can be dyed once the shells are removed and make for a gorgeous deviled egg display.

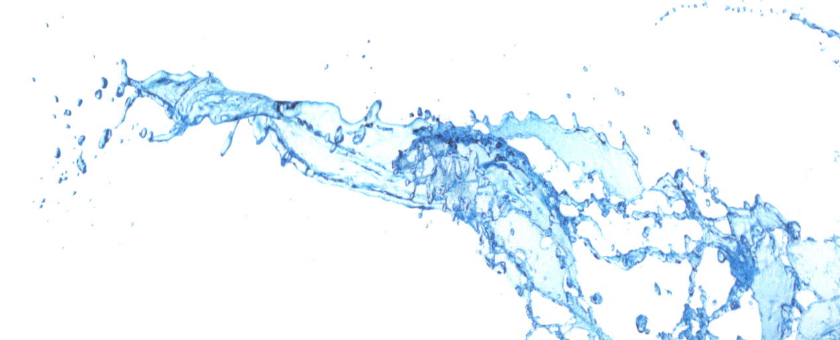

Prepare the eggs by gently lowering into a pot of boiling water and allowing to cook for 11-13 minutes (less for smaller eggs, more for larger). Remove the pot from the heat and transfer the eggs to a bowl of ice water until cool.

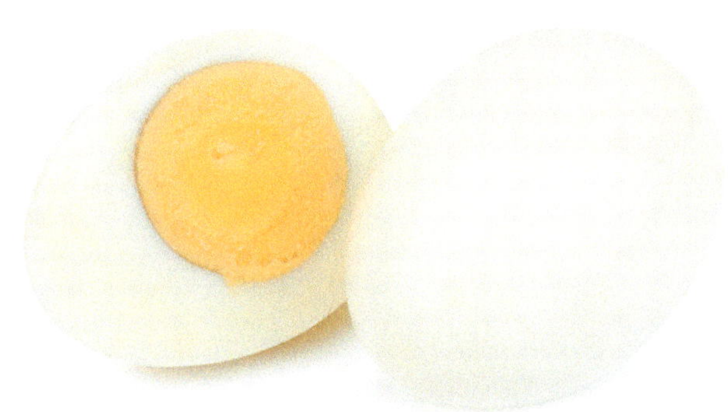

**Blow** If you want to keep your egg art indefinitely, though, you'll want to use "blown" eggs. To blow an egg:

**1** Gently clean the egg with a 50/50 dish soap and water solution using a soft towel.

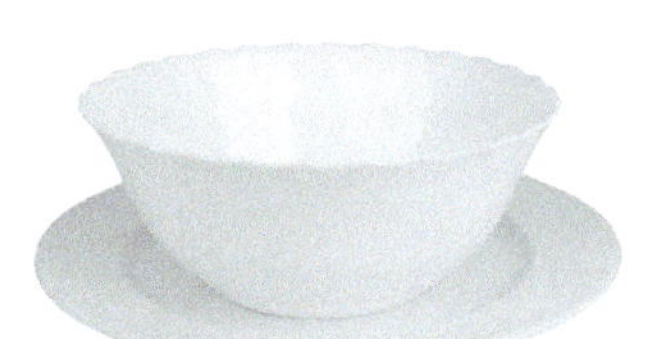

**2** Put a bowl under your egg.

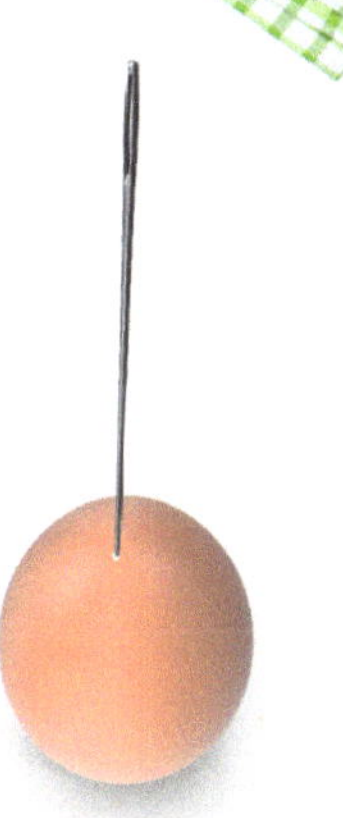

**3** Use a sewing needle carefully to poke a pinhole in the narrower end of the egg.

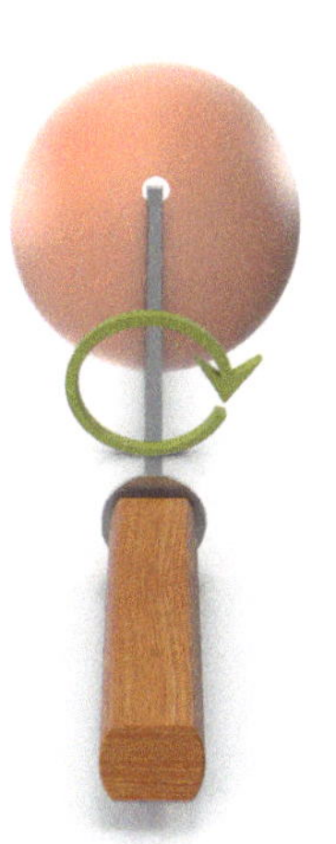

**4** Turn the egg over and poke a pinhole in that end. Spin a wood skewer in the pinhole gently to slowly expand the size of the hole in the wider end. Turn the egg back over and wipe off the pinhole with the detergent/water solution.

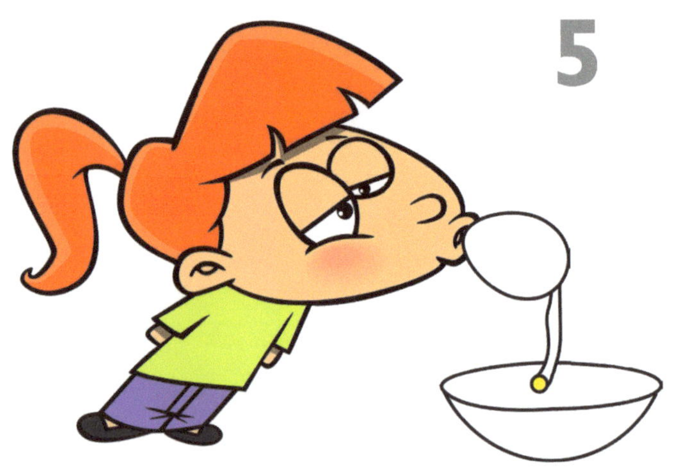

**5** Point the egg's larger hole toward the bowl, and with your mouth blow forcefully into the pinhole. The egg's contents will begin to empty out of the shell. Continue blowing until the egg has been completely emptied. (If you encounter a clog along the way, use the skewer or needle to break up any clogs or to expand the larger hole, of needed.)

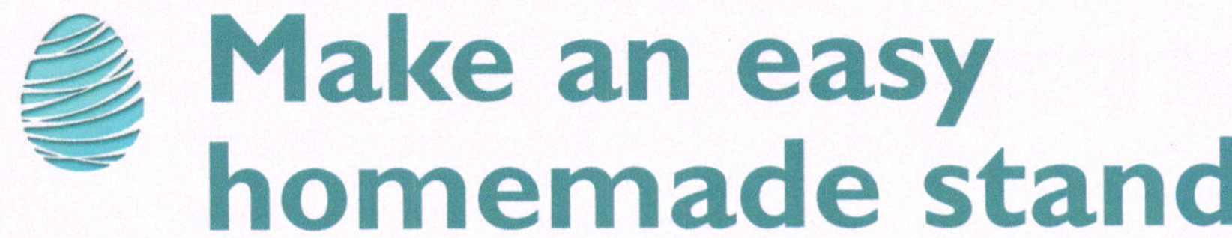

# Make an easy homemade stand

Some people are happy to use the carton their eggs came in to hold their eggs during decoration and drying, while others purchase special egg holders.

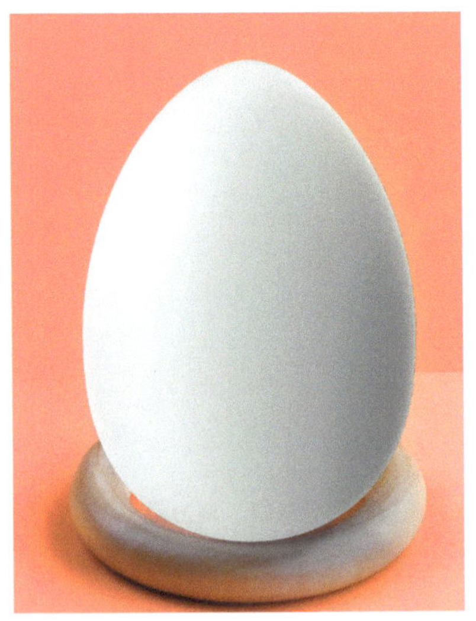

Curtain rings make a fantastic and inexpensive base for holding up an egg.

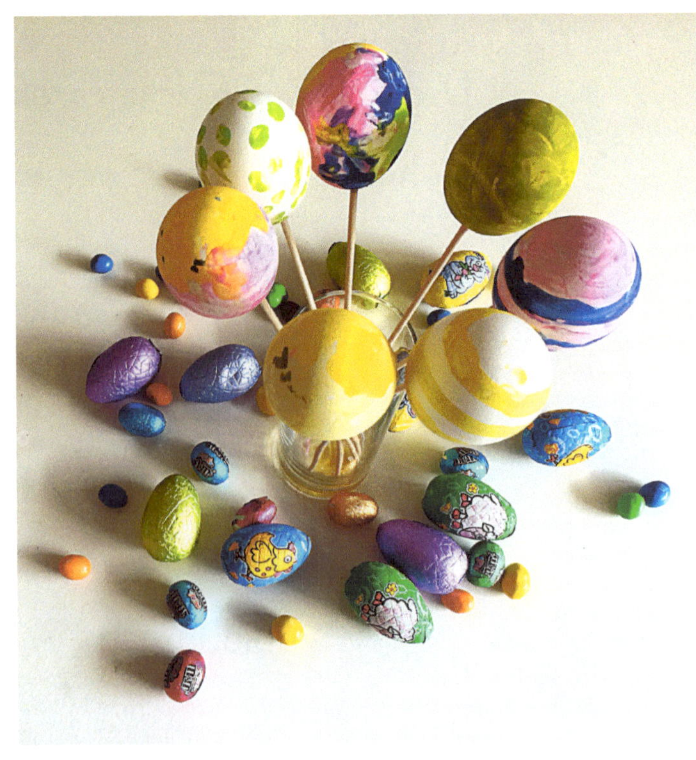

A wood skewer or fireplace match stuck into a Styrofoam egg container or narrow glass works very well to hold up a blown egg.

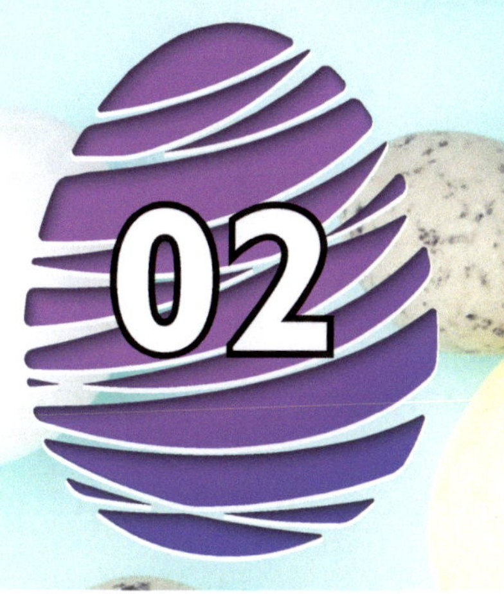



# Make a dye bath and dip your eggs

- use food coloring to make a dye bath
- make your own natural dyes
- dipping & simple variations

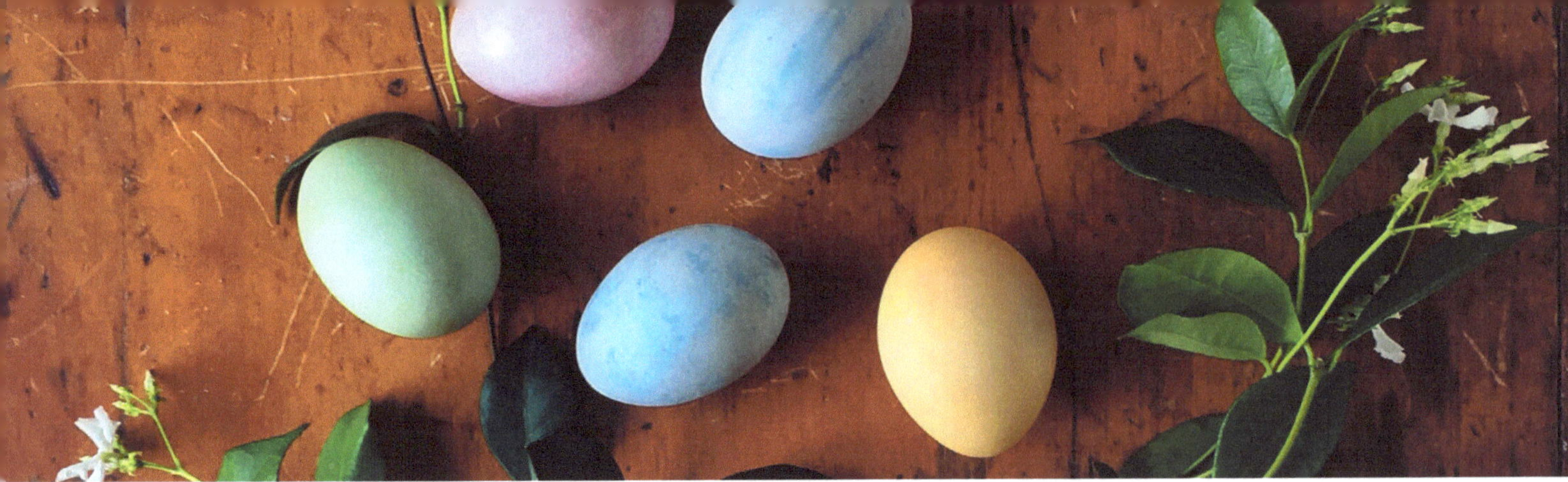

Nothing says Easter like a basketful of dyed eggs.

Even the most innovative decorators often start by dipping their eggs in dye, since it provides a rich and saturated overall canvas. Others dye with a twist in order to make marbled eggs. Some decorators paint their designs in dye instead of using acrylic or gouache paints (see chapter 4).

There's even a specialized kind of traditional egg dyeing that uses onion skins, leaves, and flowers with natural dyes to create breathtaking botanical egg designs (see chapter 3).

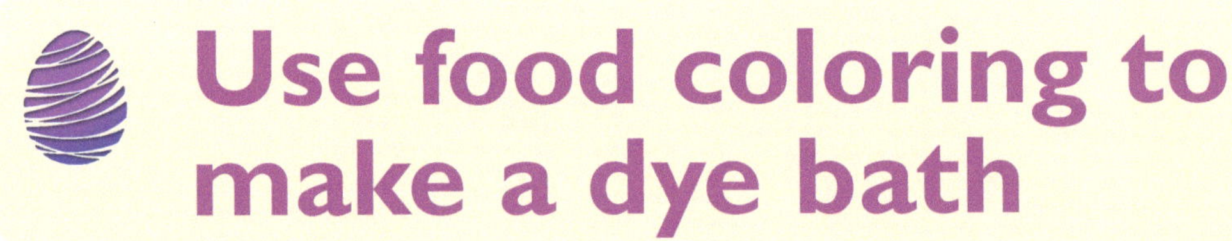

## Use food coloring to make a dye bath

An easy way to make a dye bath is to mix ½ cup boiling water with 10-20 drops of food coloring (using a single color or mixing different colors) and 1 tsp vinegar in a cup.

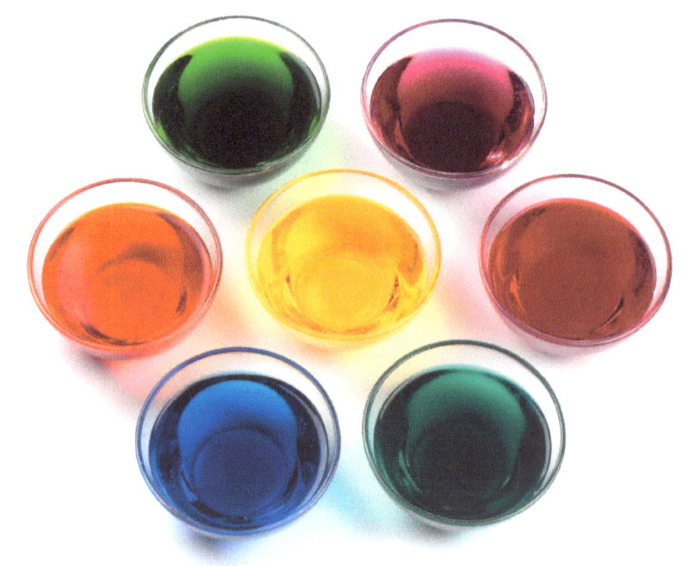

# Make your own natural dyes

If you want to be truly creative—and avoid artificial colors—you'll find that it's easy to make your own natural dyes. Just be aware that eggs often need to soak longer in a natural dye bath than they would in an artificial one to achieve the desired depth of color.

## Base Recipe

Bring 1 cup water plus the desired coloring agent (see right) to boil in a saucepan.

Reduce heat and simmer for 15-30 minutes.

Cool. Strain and add 2 tsp of distilled white vinegar.

| Color | Add |
|---|---|
| Pink | 1 cup of chopped beets |
| Blue | 1 cup frozen blueberries |
| Green | 1 cup spinach |
| Brown | 1/4 cup coffee grounds |
| Orange | 2 tsp turmeric powder |
| Yellow | 2 tsp cumin powder or 1 orange peel |

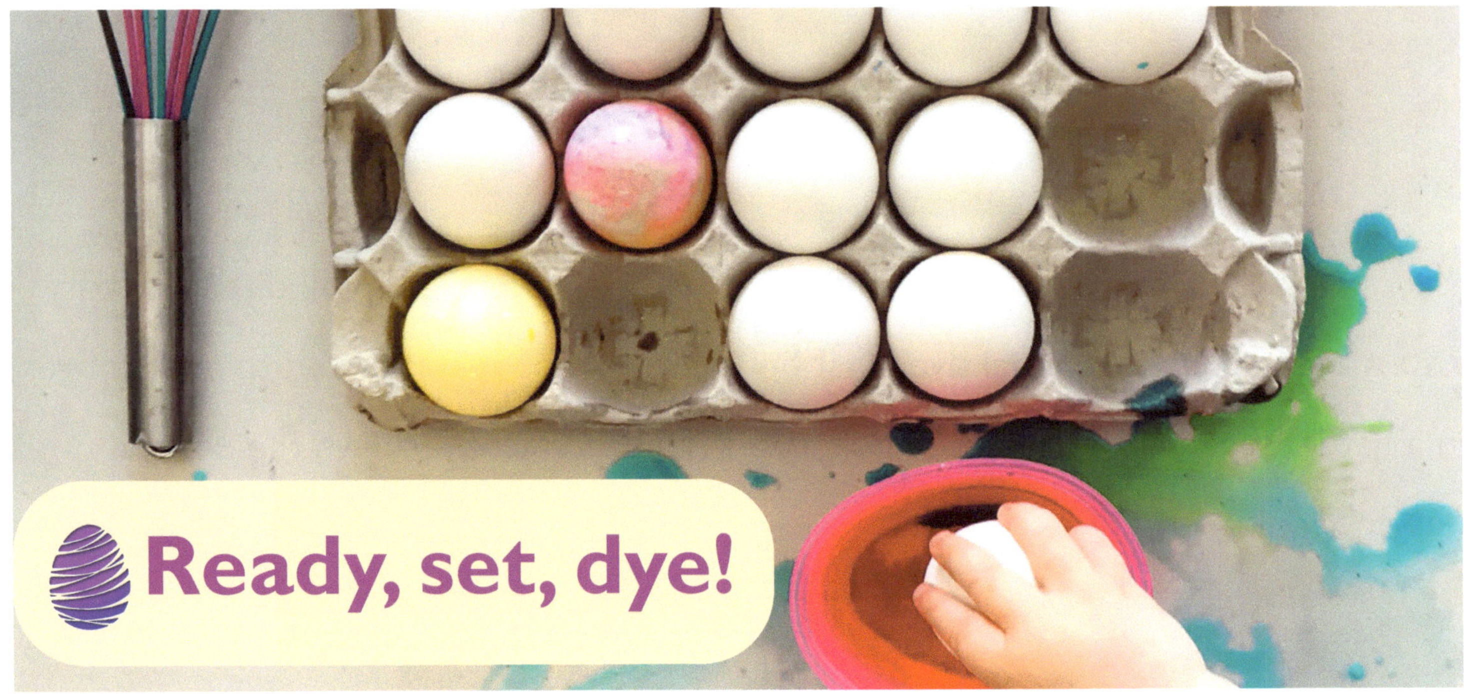



Set up each color dye bath in a cup sized to allow an egg to be fully submerged.

## For solid-color

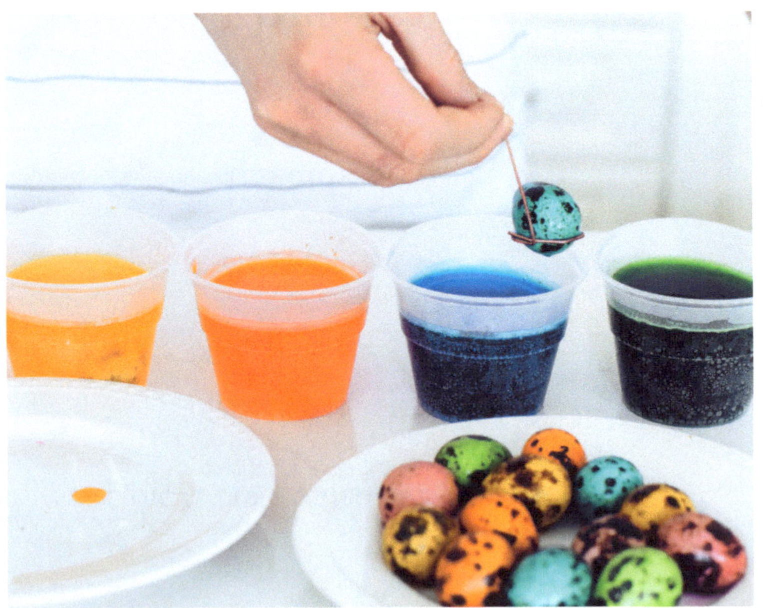

Slide an egg into the bath (or hold the egg partially submerged, if you don't want the color all over). Let it sit for 5-30 minutes (usually shorter for artificial dyes, longer for natural dyes). Remove using a slotted spoon, tongs, or wire egg holder and place on stand to dry.

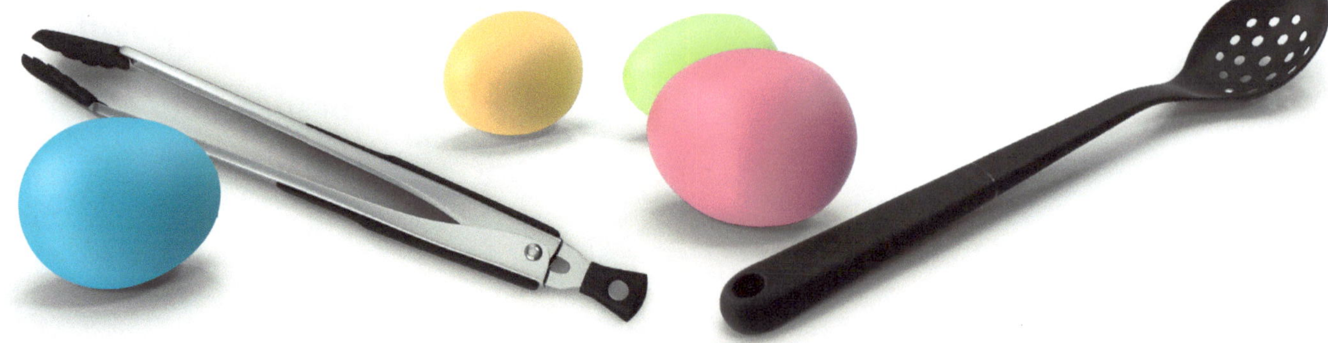

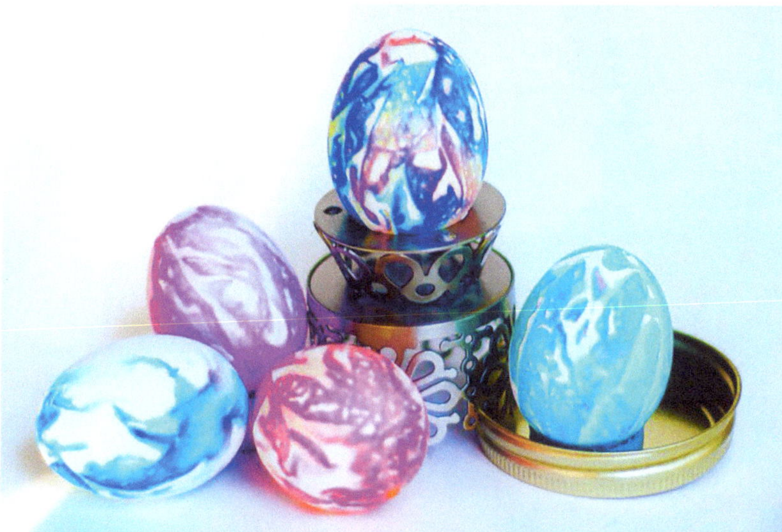

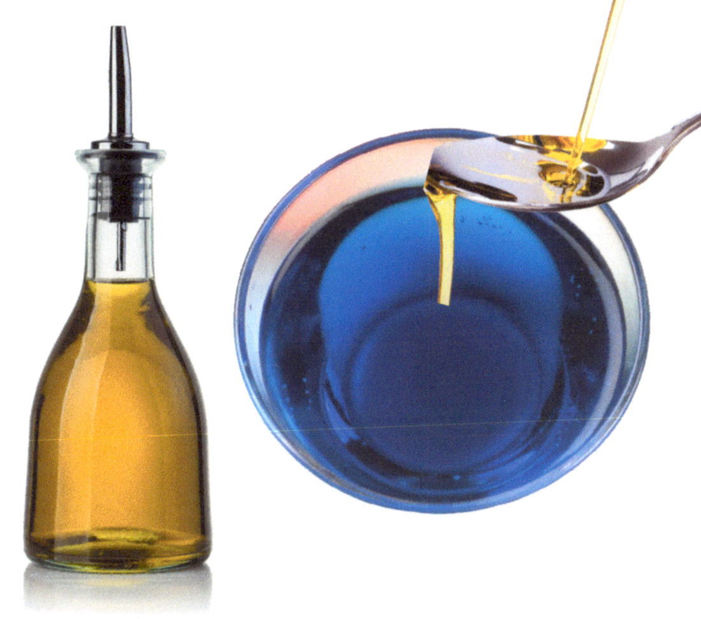

Before dipping your egg, swirl 1 tsp of olive oil into the dye bath. Then use a spoon to roll the egg gently in the dye, streaking it with color. Remove and blot on a towel. Repeat in other colors, if a multi-colored effect is desired.

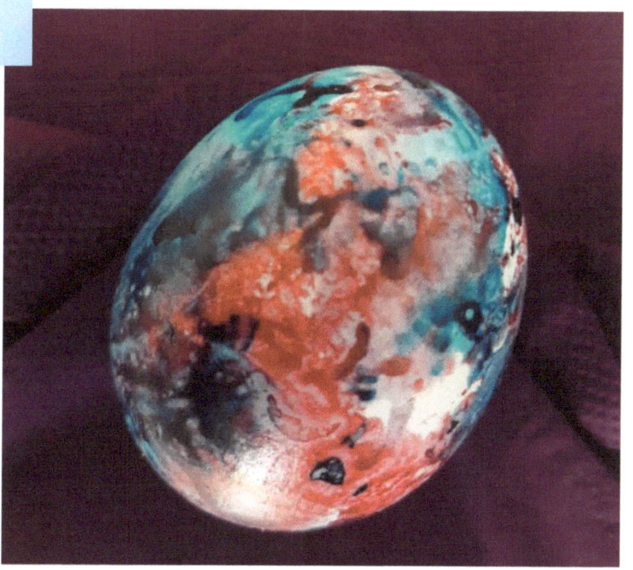



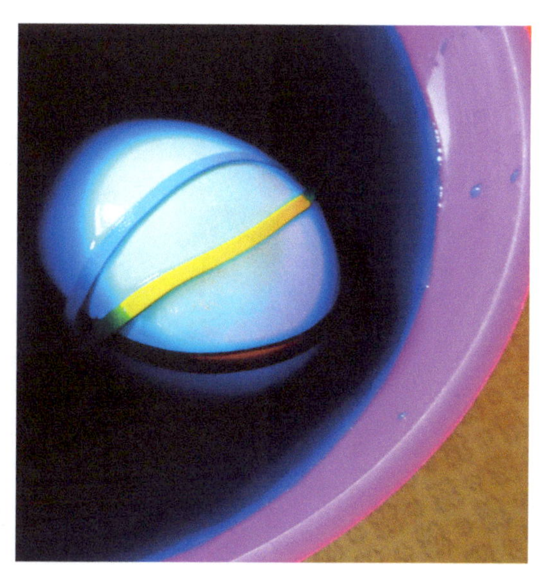

Put rubber bands around your egg where you want stripes to appear, then dip the egg into the dye.

For more colorful stripes, start with an egg that's already been dyed and allowed to dry.

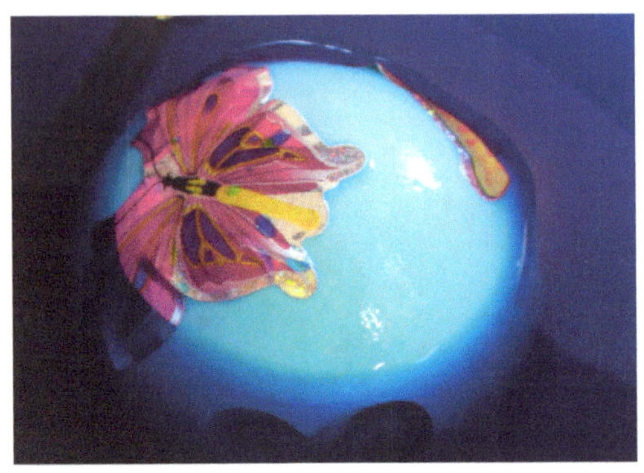



Before you dip your egg, adhere small vinyl (water resistant) stickers to it.

Remove the stickers after the egg dries, and the shape of the stickers will be left behind.

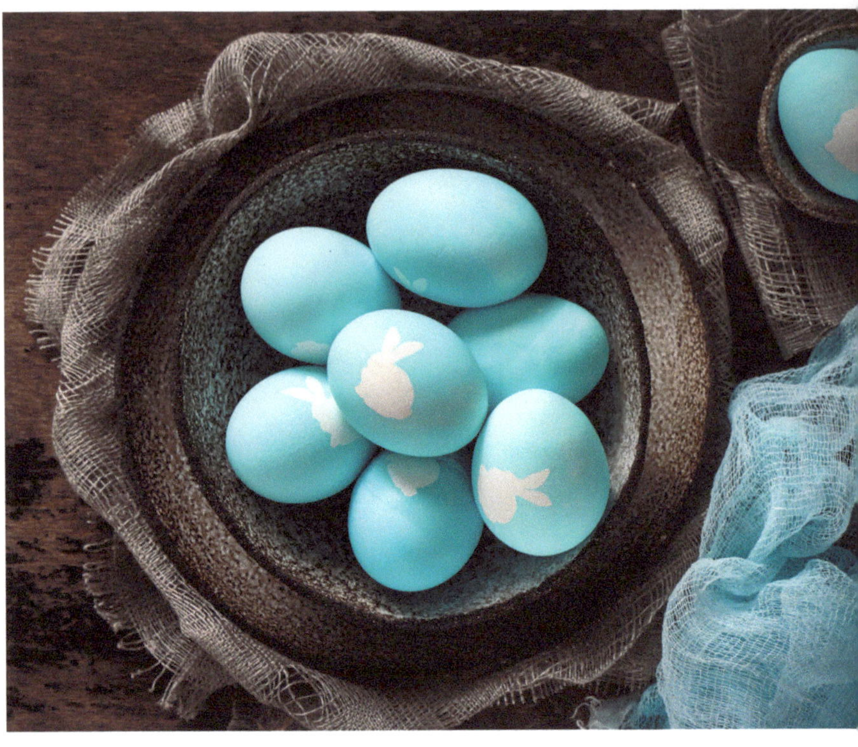

Make a splash with dyed eggs!

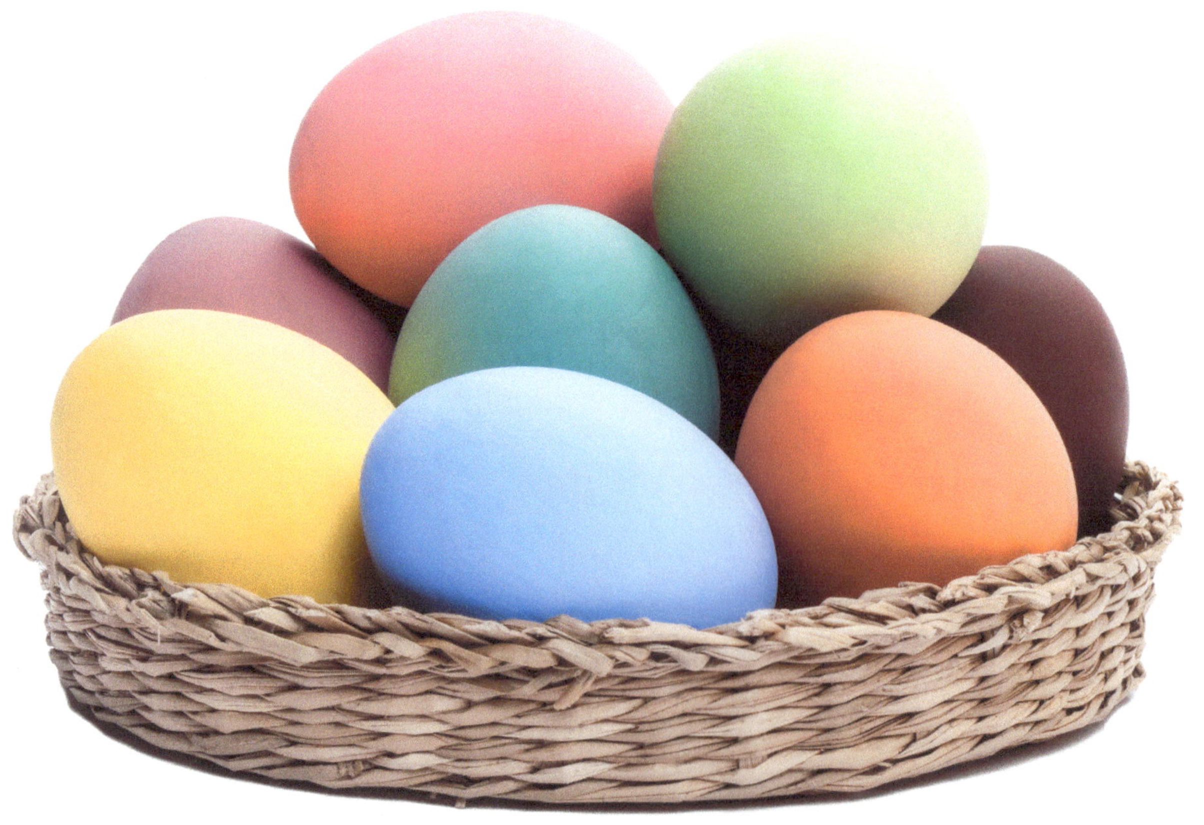

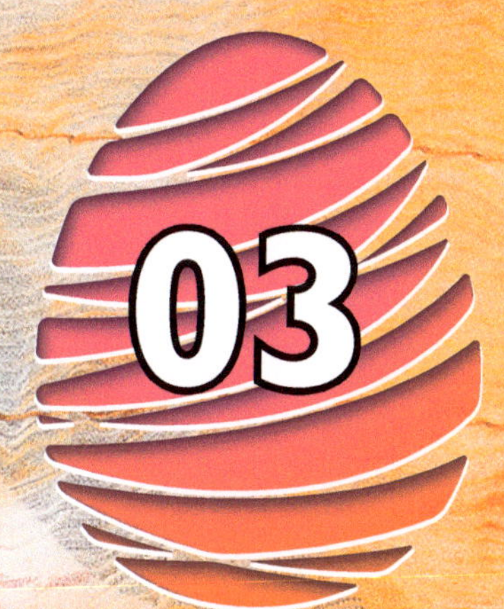

# 03

Use onion skins, leaves and flowers to make traditional dyed eggs

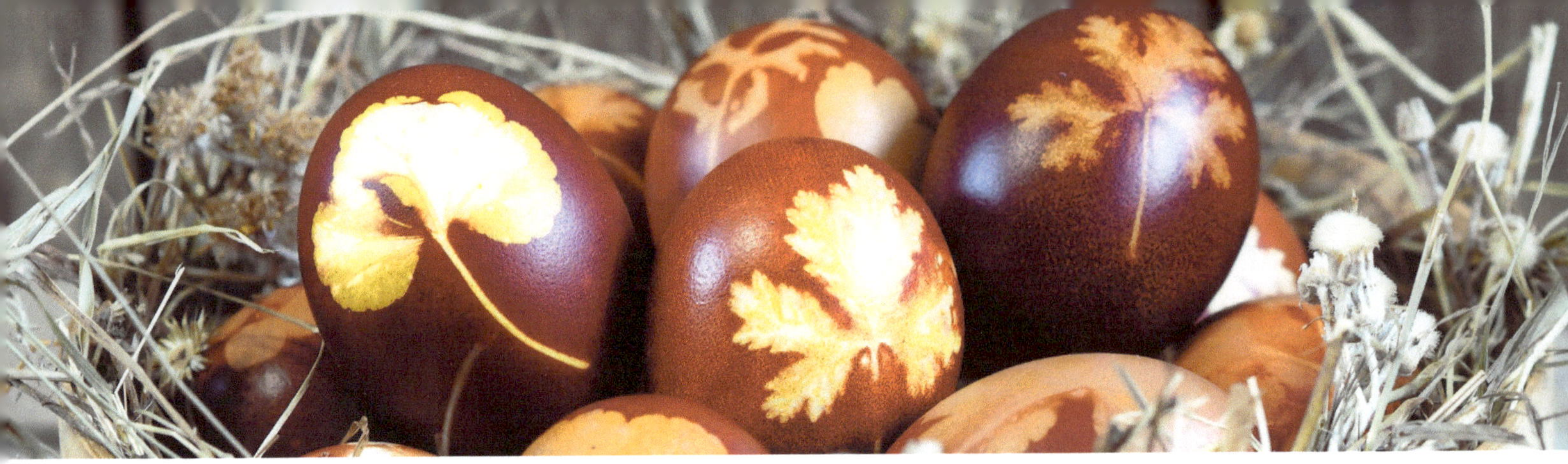

Before there were egg-dyeing kits and artificial dyes aplenty, people outside the United States routinely practiced a traditional form of egg-dying to celebrate the start of spring. Subtler, less uniform, and bearing the marks of leaves and flowers, onion-skin-dyed eggs connect us both to the past and to the abundance of the natural world around us.

No two eggs will be alike, but all will possess a subtle beauty and the artful strokes of nature.

## Collect the ingredients you'll need

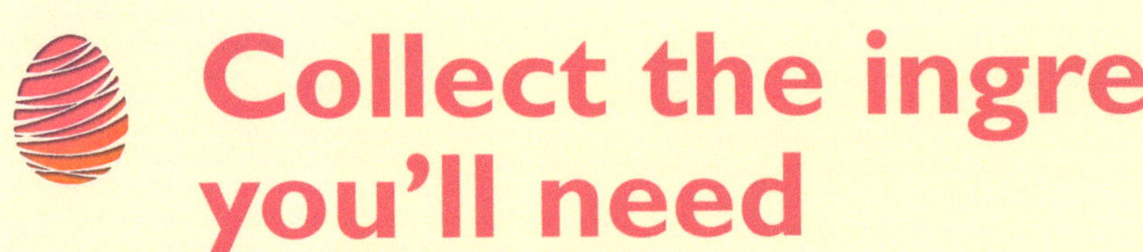

Head outdoors and collect fresh fern fronds, small leaves, grasses, and flowers. Pansies, crocuses, and hyacinths are flowers that work especially well.

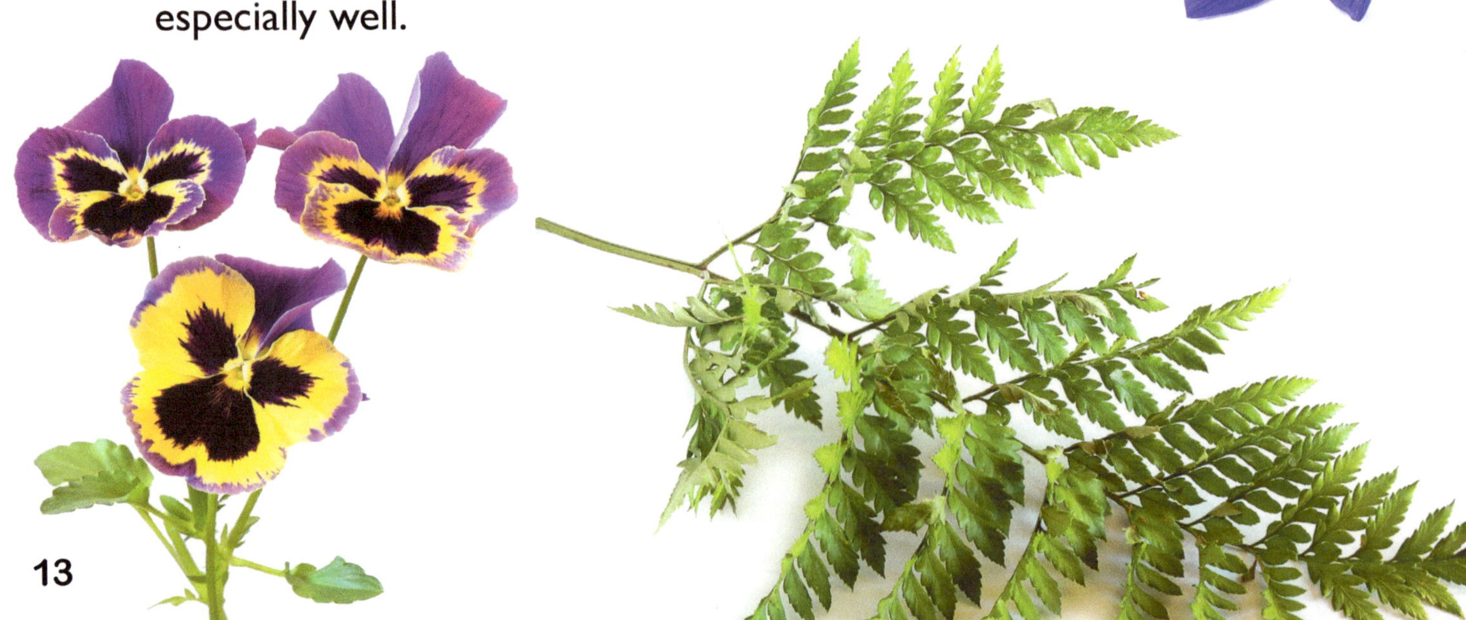

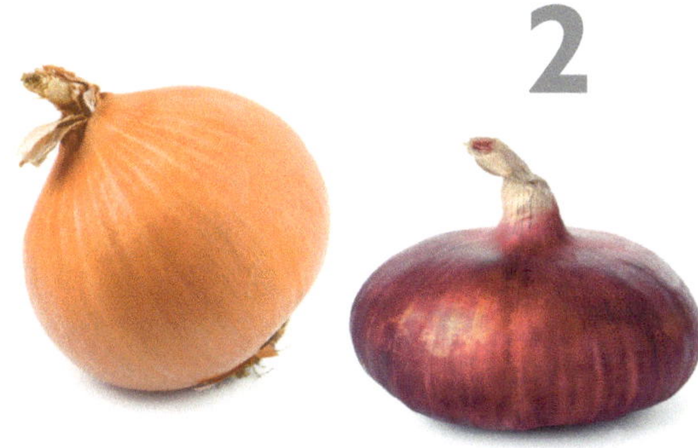

**2** Gather the papery, outer skins from red or yellow onions–you'll need about 2 per egg. The more skins you use, the deeper the color will be. Red will result in a pinkish-brown coloration, while yellow will create a beige-light yellow color.

**3** One 6x6 inch piece of thin cloth or sturdy paper towel per egg

**4** Twine, twist ties, or rubber bands

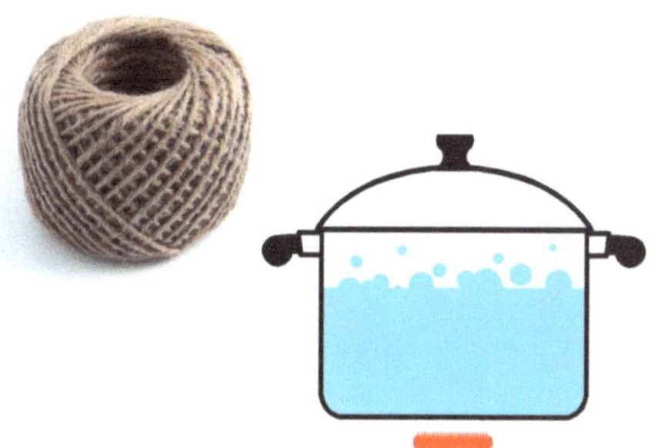

**5** A large pot of boiling water

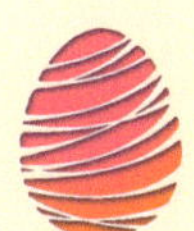 # Prepare each egg

**1** Moisten your ferns, leaves, grasses, and flowers and wrap them all around the egg

**2** Wrap two onion skins around the covered egg

**3** Wrap the egg in the cloth or paper towel

**4** Seal with twine, twist ties, or rubber bands

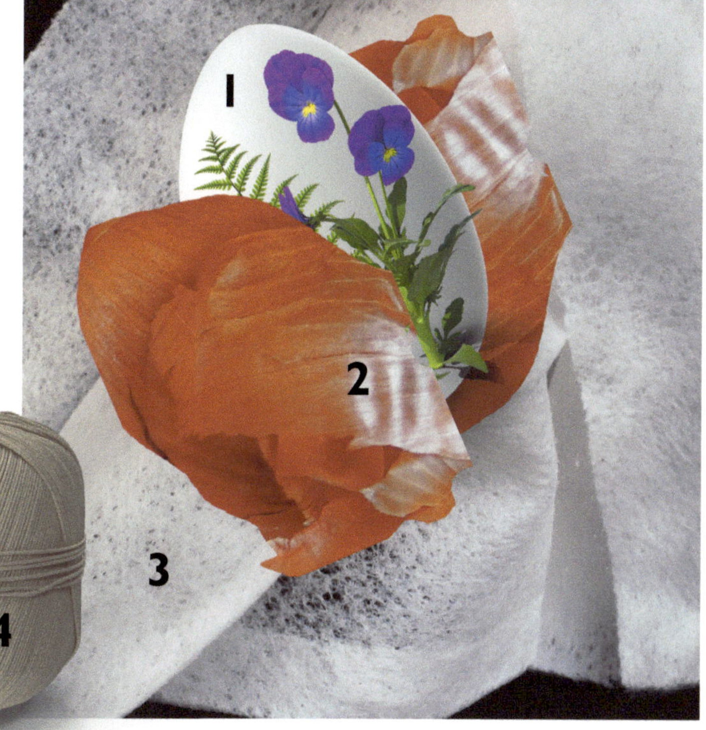

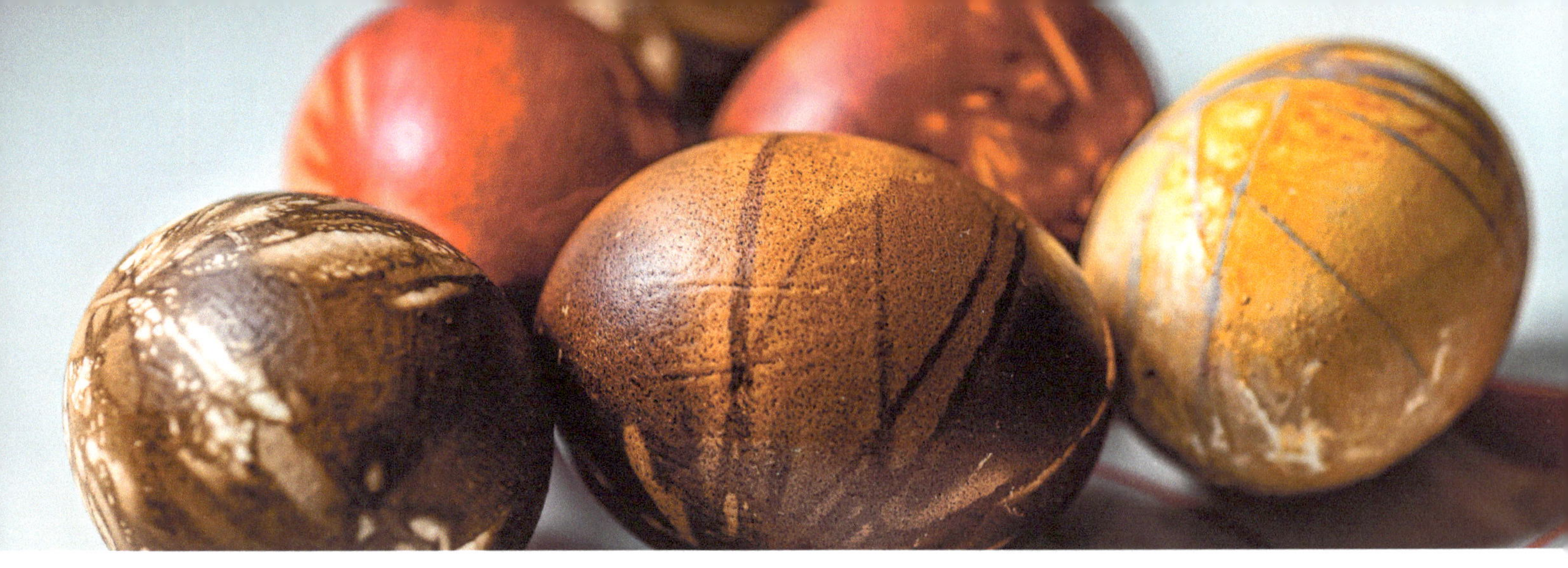



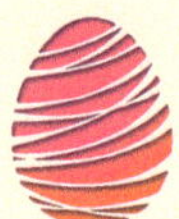

## Boil the prepared eggs

1   Drop each egg carefully into the boiling water

2   After 10 minutes, remove the eggs and allow to cool, then unwrap the eggs and admire the beautiful imprinted shapes of greenery and subtle splashes of color left behind by the flowers

3   If desired, use a small piece of cloth to rub vegetable oil on the eggs – this will give them a slightly glossy finish

## A more colorful variation

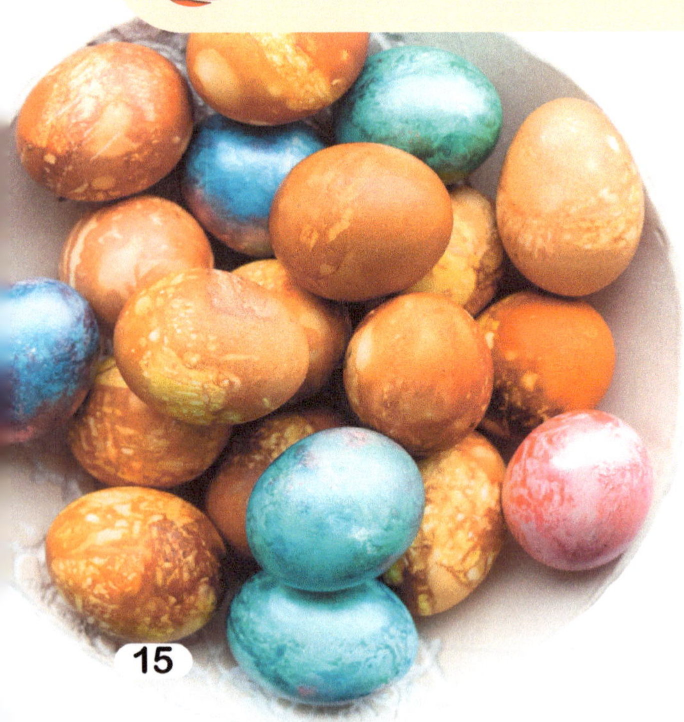

If you'd like to imbue your eggs with a different background color, omit the onion skins and instead infuse your boiling water with the natural dye ingredients in the proportions listed in chapter 2. Boil the eggs for about 30 minutes – longer for a deeper coloration, shorter for more subtlety.

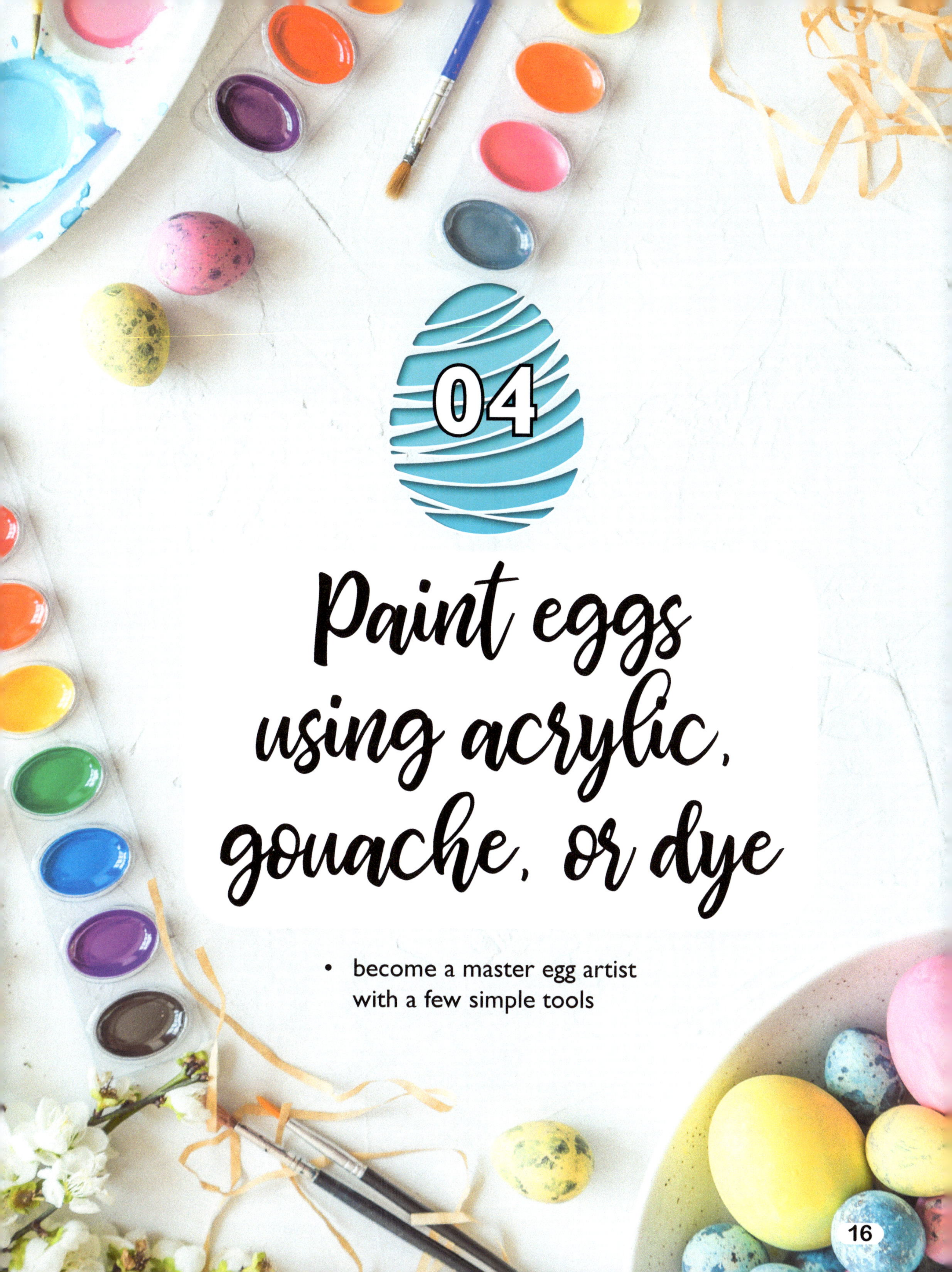
04
Paint eggs using acrylic, gouache, or dye
become a master egg artist with a few simple tools
16

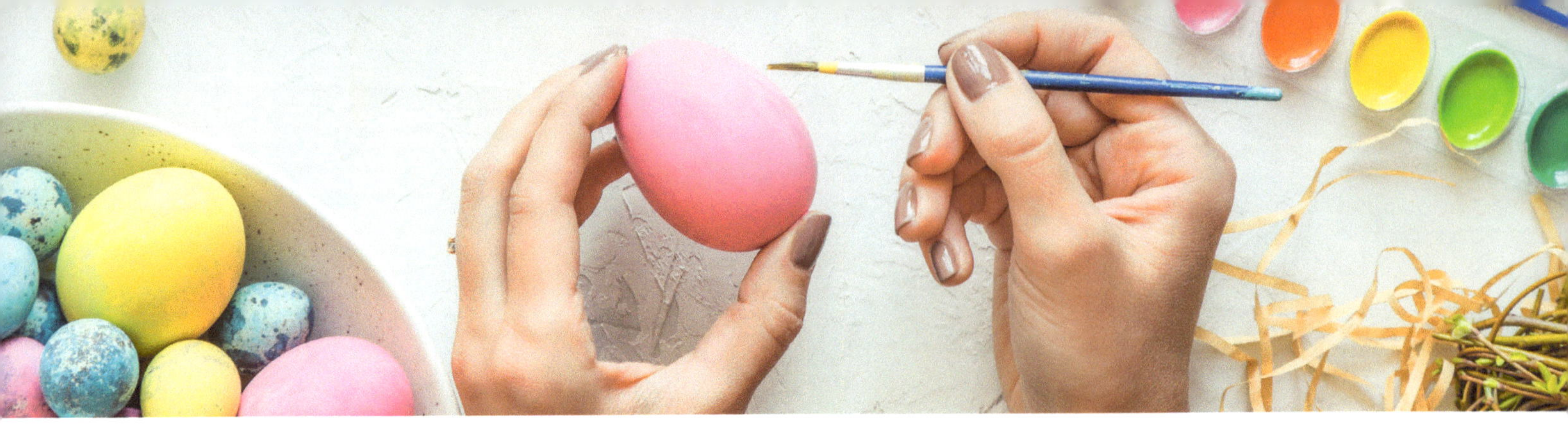

Painting your egg with a brush will allow you to be the ultimate egg master-artist. You can choose your own abstract, geometric, realistic, calligraphic, or painterly style and create nearly any special effect you desire. You're limited only by your own imagination!

Just remember, if you are using hard-boiled eggs that might be eaten later, be sure to use only non-toxic paints and dyes.

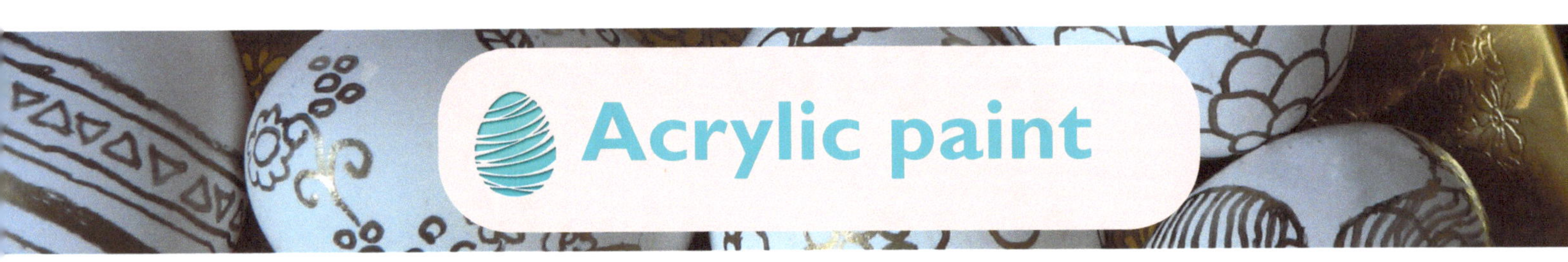

# Acrylic paint

Acrylic paints are the easiest to work with and adhere well to the surface of an eggshell.

They are opaque and available in non-toxic formulations and a virtually limitless variety of colors, including neons and metallics.

Use acrylic paint if you want to be able to paint layers over other layers without muddying the colors.

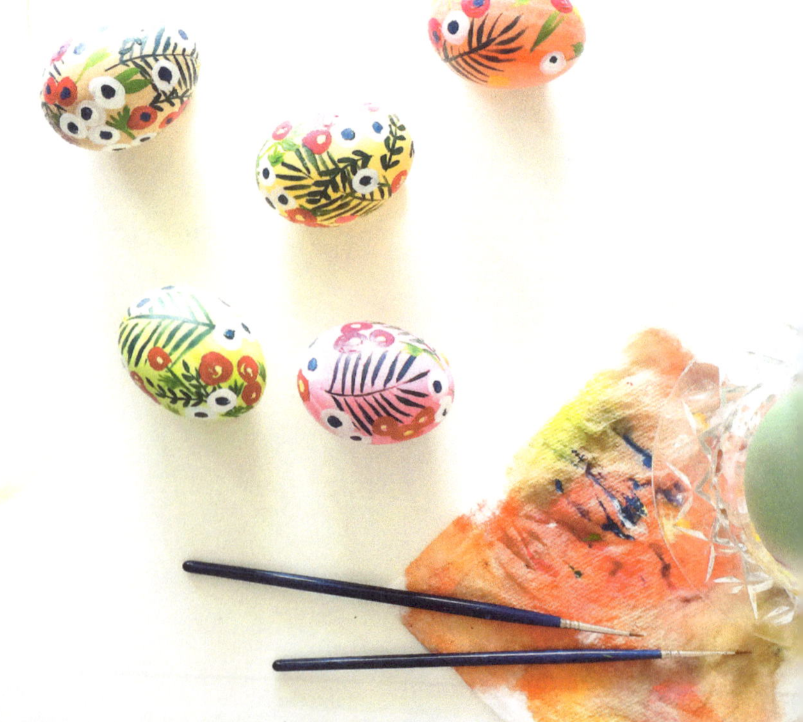

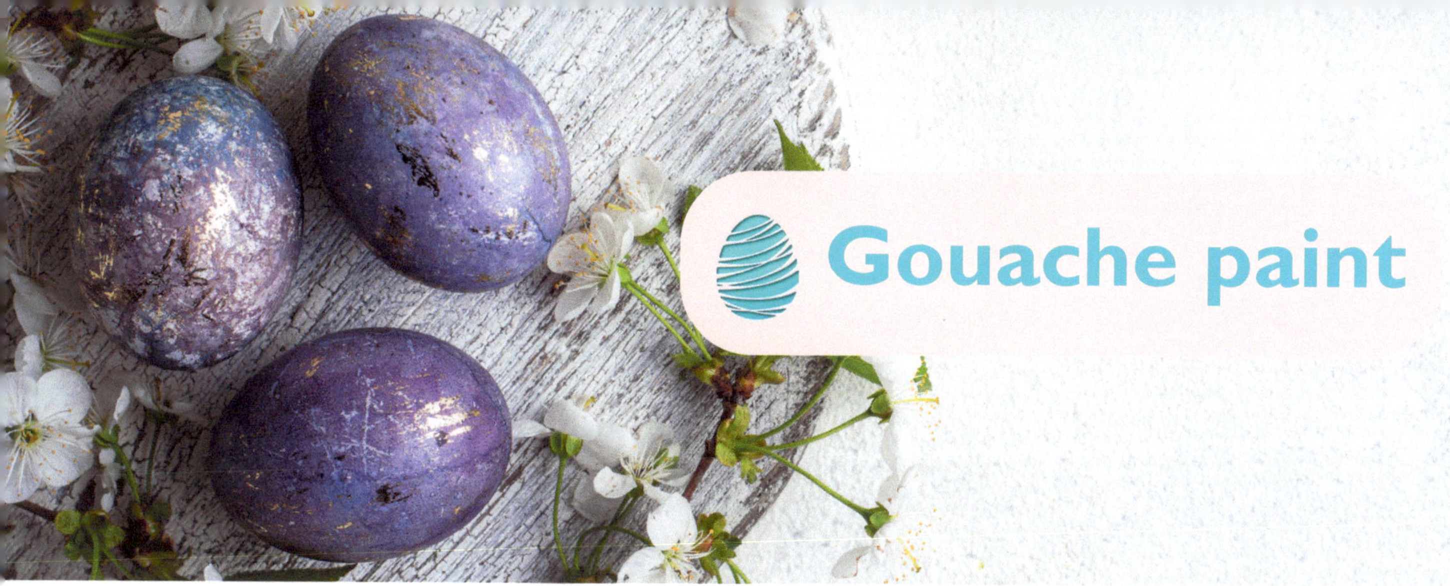

# Gouache paint

*G*ouache paint is an opaque, watercolor-like paint that places pigment on the surface of the egg. Often, artists water down gouache paints (creating a wash) to make them easier to work with while maintaining much of their opacity.

You can create gorgeous effects with gouache, especially when painting plants or flowers, but colors can get muddy if you paint over them with different colors. Specialty gouache paints containing an acrylic binder are also available and mitigate this undesired effect.

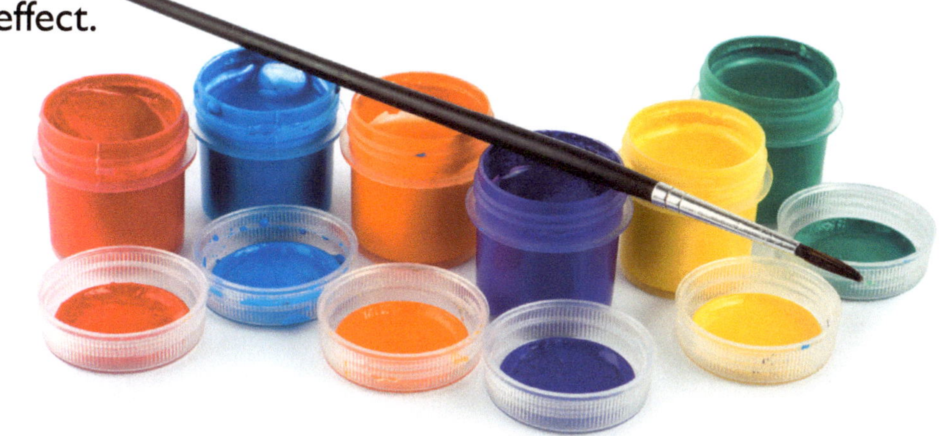

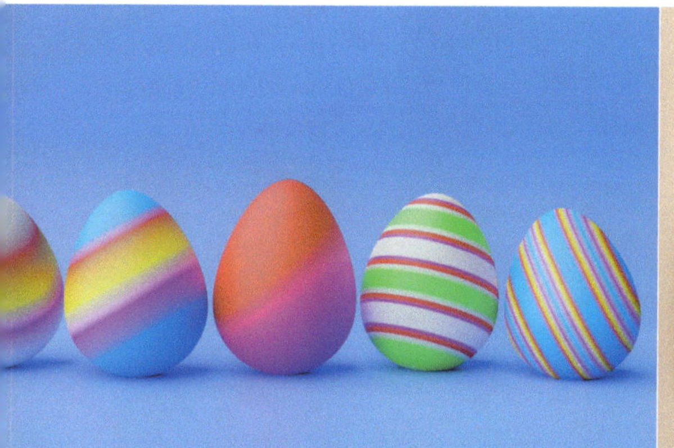

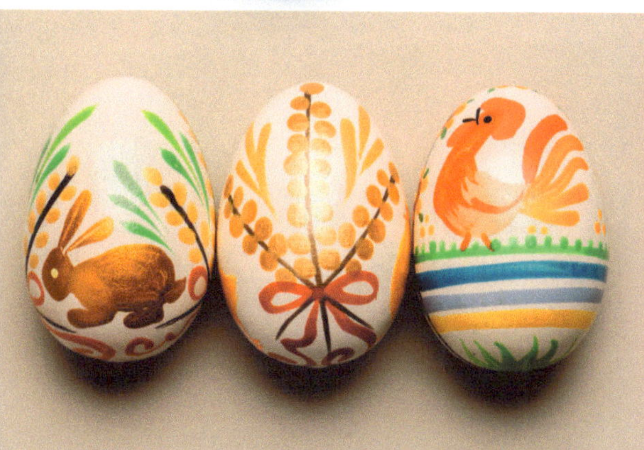

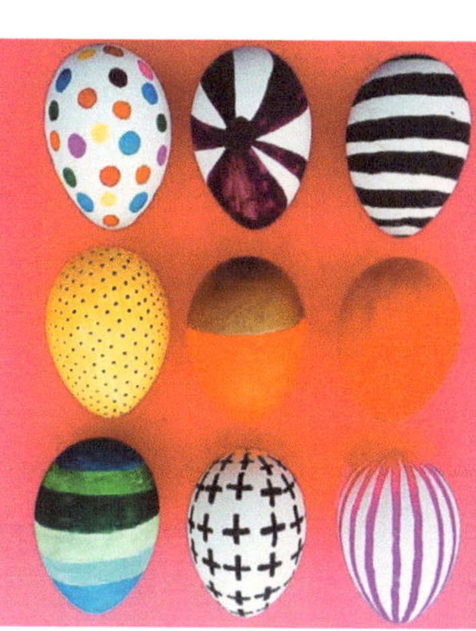

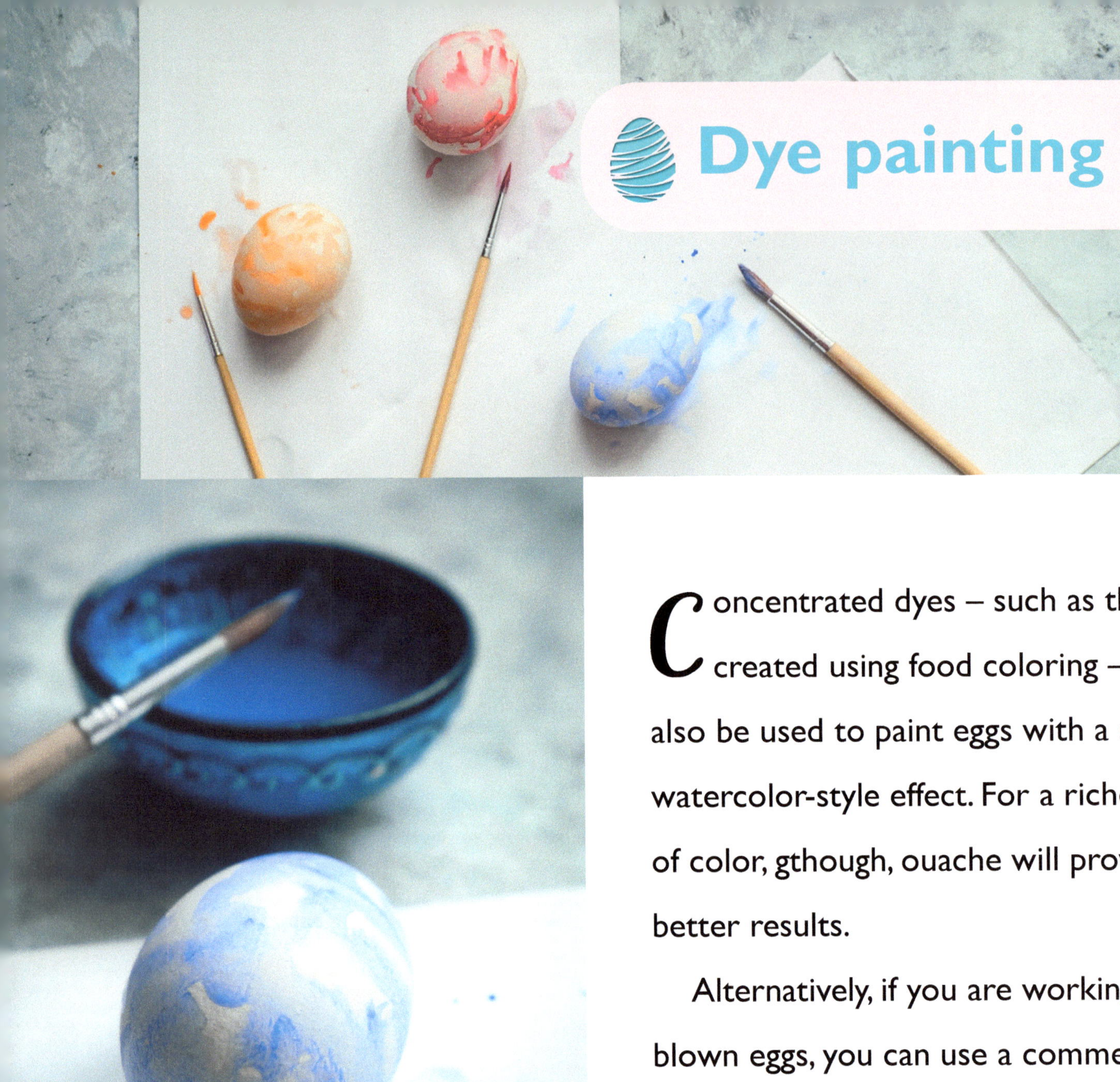



*C*oncentrated dyes – such as those created using food coloring – can also be used to paint eggs with a subtle watercolor-style effect. For a richer depth of color, gthough, ouache will provide better results.

Alternatively, if you are working with blown eggs, you can use a commercial fabric dye to achieve deeper colors.

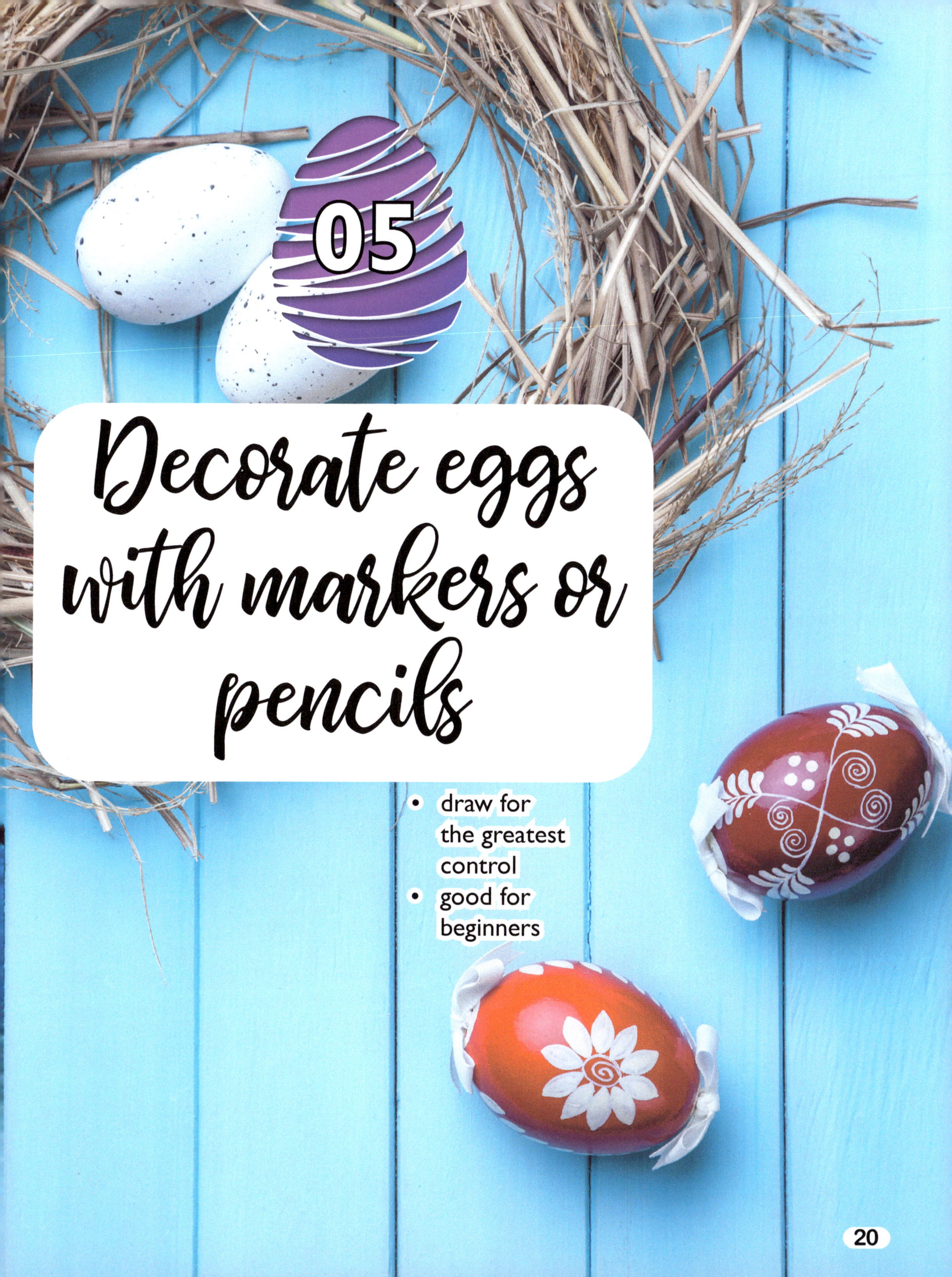

# 05

# Decorate eggs with markers or pencils

- draw for the greatest control
- good for beginners

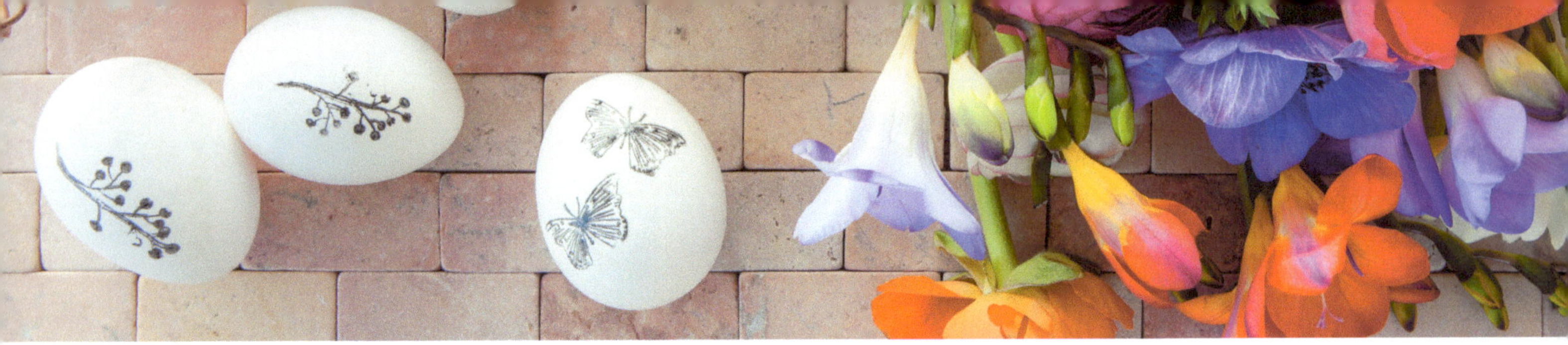

For precise control over your designs, use markers or pencils. These tools make egg decorating a snap!

##  Acrylic markers 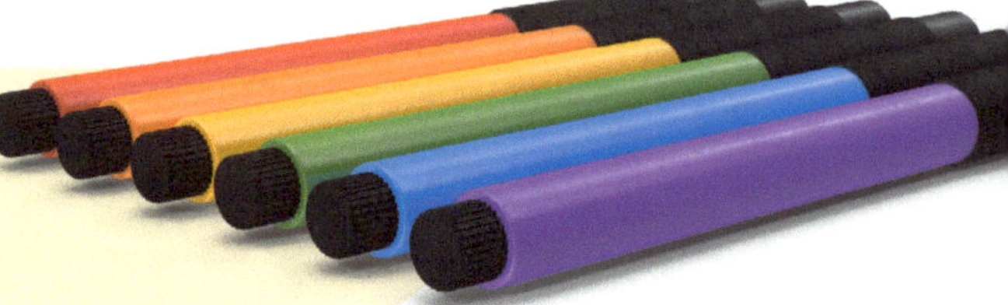

Acrylic markers give the most paint-like results and are available in a range of thicknesses, from fine to chunky, and a variety of vibrant and iridescent colors. Choose nontoxic markers if using hard-boiled eggs that might be eaten later.

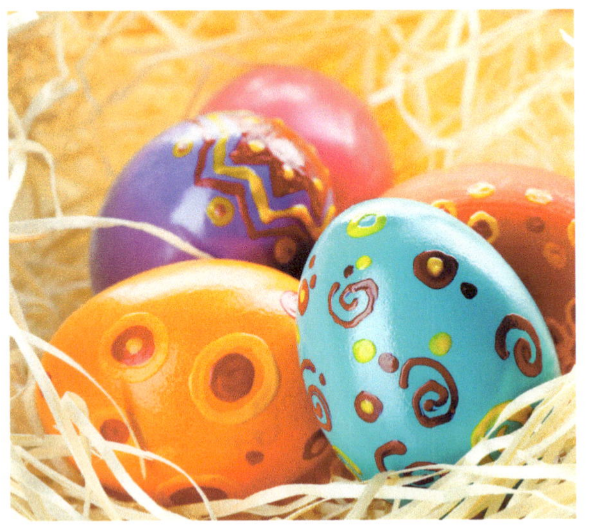

Before you use the marker, give it a good shake to ensure even mixing. Then, press the nib (tip) of the marker down on a piece of scrap paper a few times to get the flow going. When you finish using the marker, be sure to cap it. Let your egg dry to avoid smudging the wet acrylic.

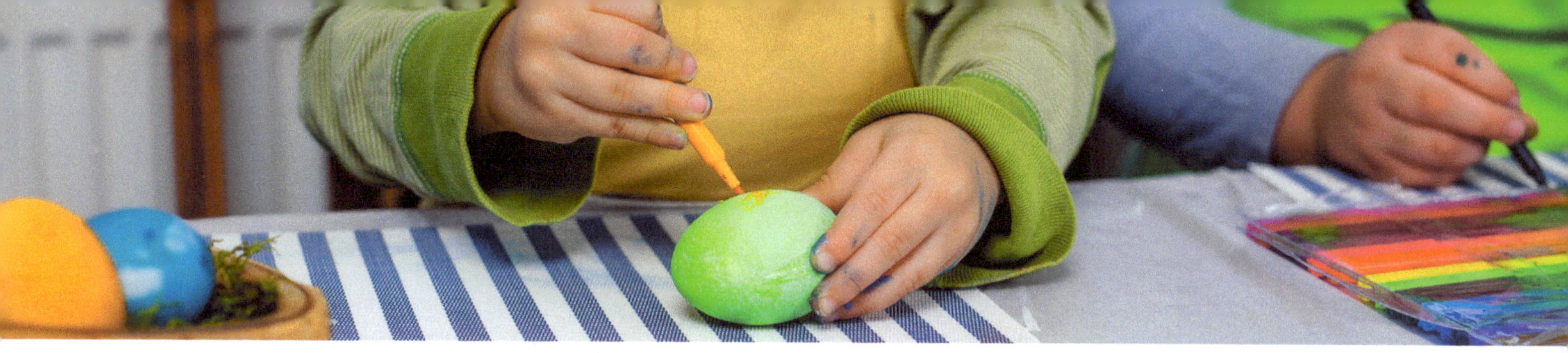

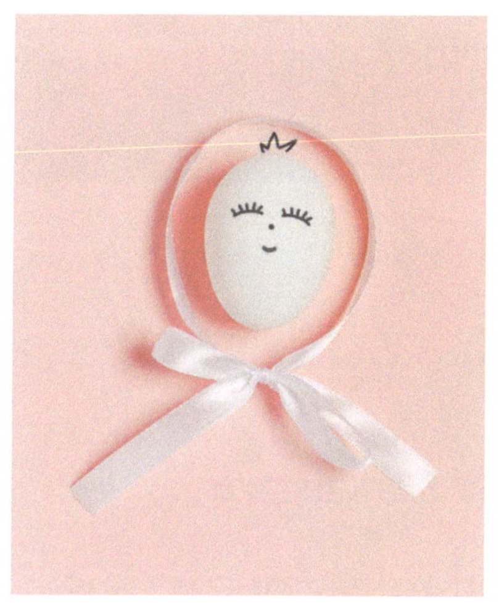

 # Permanent markers

**P**ermanent markers can also be used on eggshells. Some commercial manufacturers make non-toxic permanent markers specifically formulated for egg decorating. Choose non-toxic markers for hard-cooked eggs.

As with acrylic, allow the ink time to dry before handling the egg.

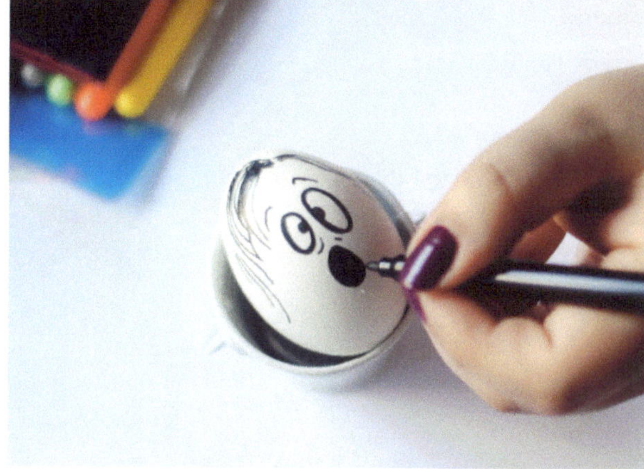

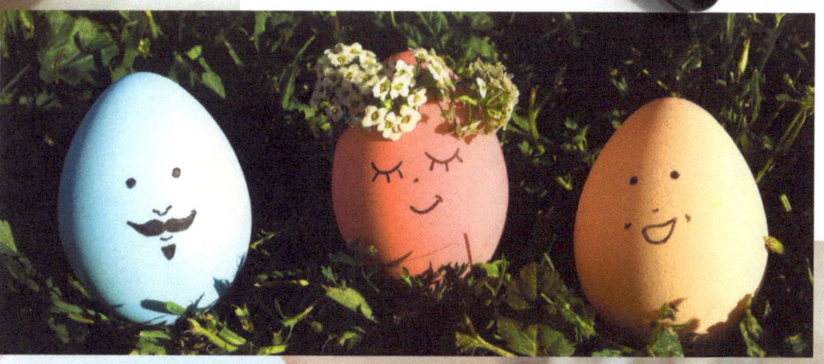



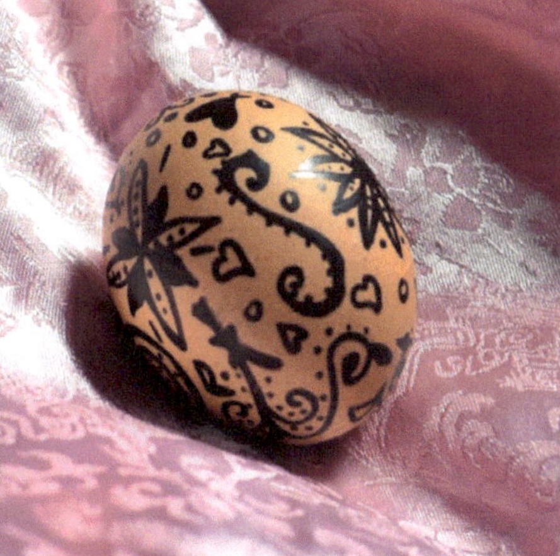

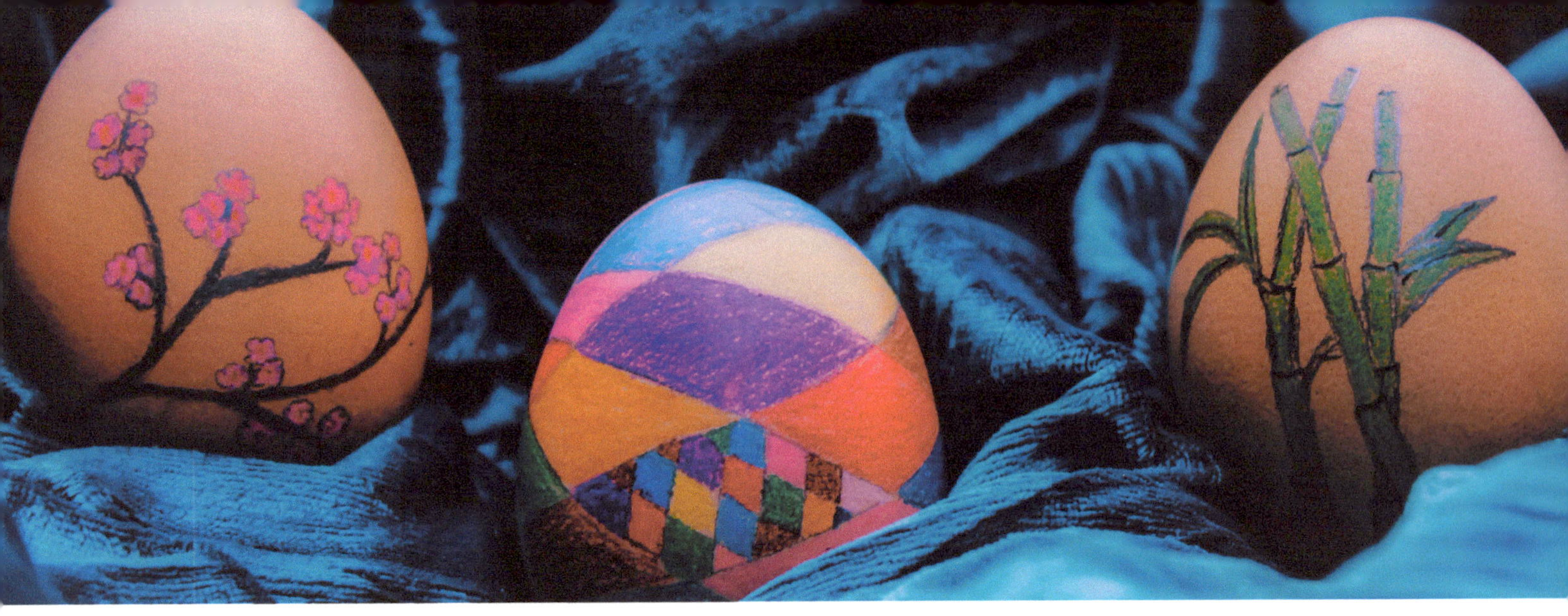



## 🥚 Colored pencils

Not all colored pencils are equally suited to egg decorating because of the shell's smooth surface. Pencils that don't use wax as an emollient tend to adhere better than conventional wax-based pencils.

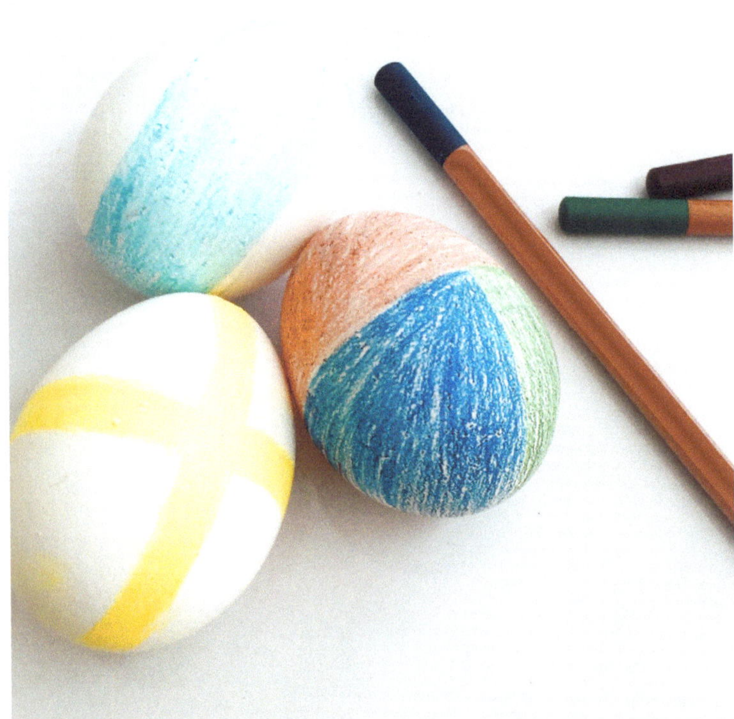

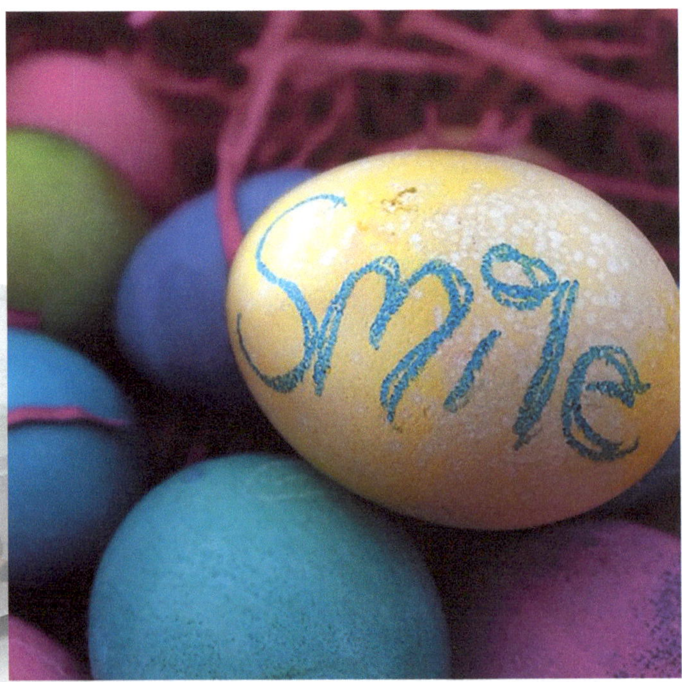

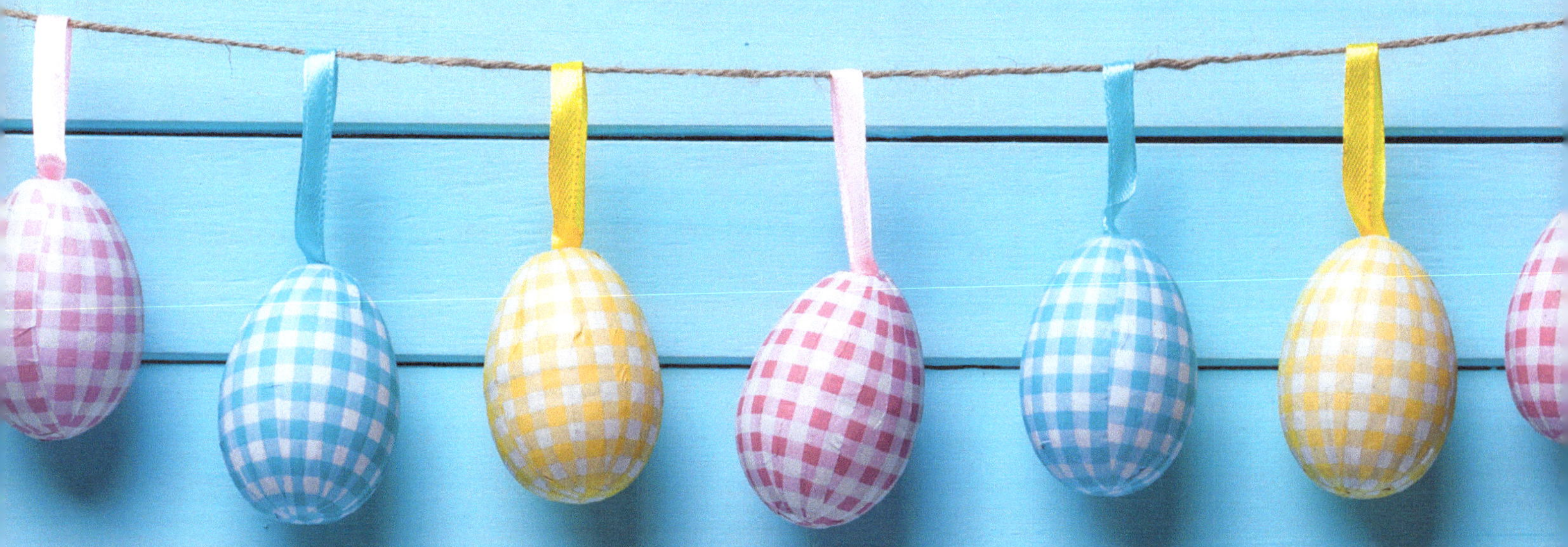

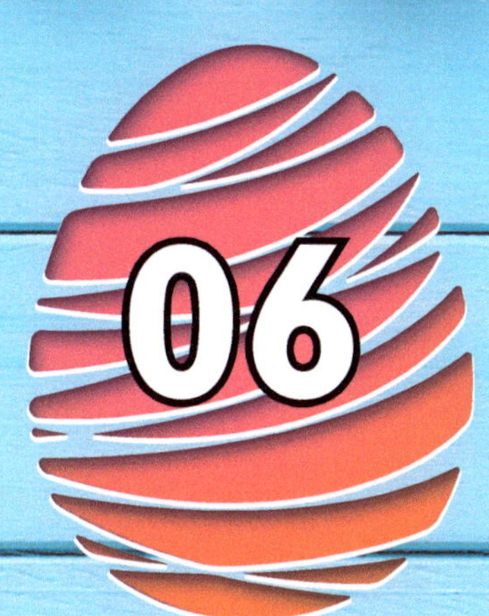

# 06

# Decorate eggs using decoupage

- create a collage egg
- add dimension
- make mosaic designs with broken egg shells

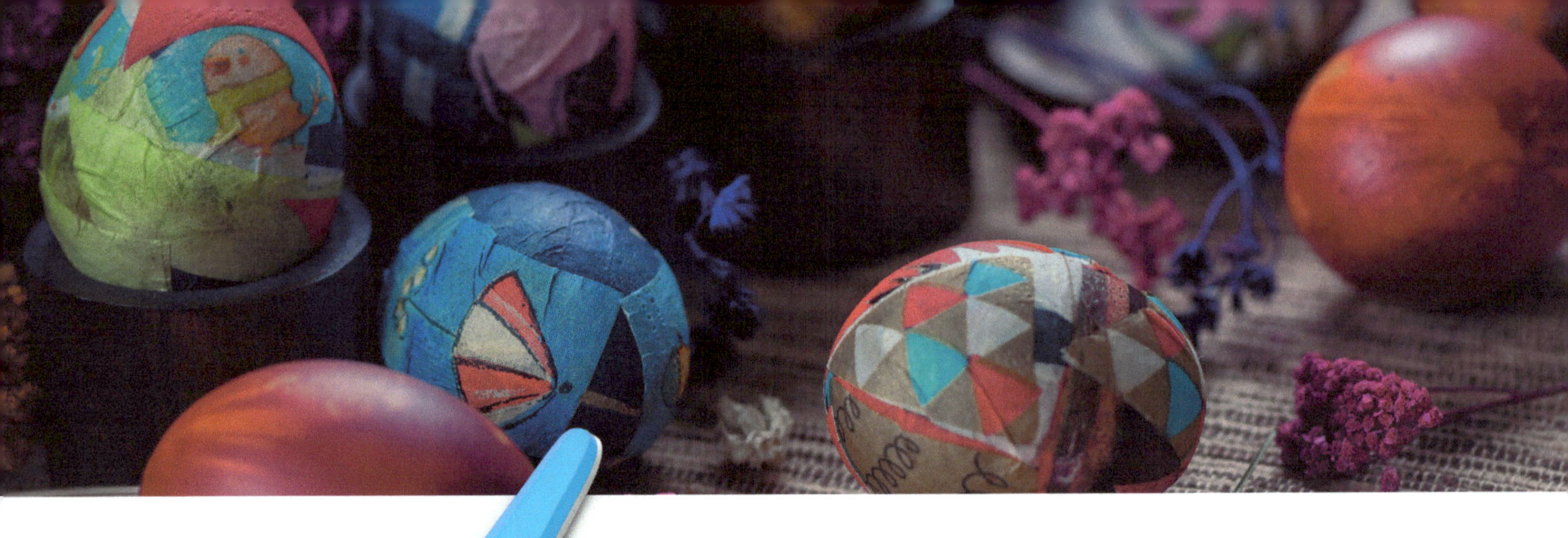

In decoupage, an artist uses glue to adhere paper to a hard surface—like an eggshell! Small clippings of thin paper can be used to create unique, colorful eggs, including complex collages that cover the entire surface of the egg.

## 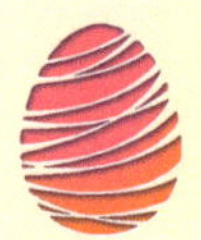 Create a collage egg

1 Cut out shapes from magazines, wrapping paper, or tissue paper.

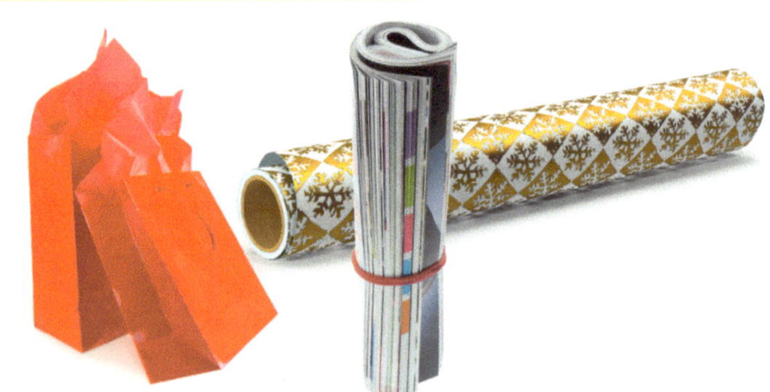

2 Brush non-toxic decoupage glue onto the back of each shape and adhere to the eggshell, smoothing out. If you are decorating a blown egg that will not be eaten later, you can instead use wallpaper paste or a watered-down craft glue (1 tablespoon of glue + 3 tablespoons of water). Keep the pieces of paper from overlapping if you want to ensure a smooth finish.

**3** After the glue dries completely, you can use a non-toxic decoupage sealer to protect it.

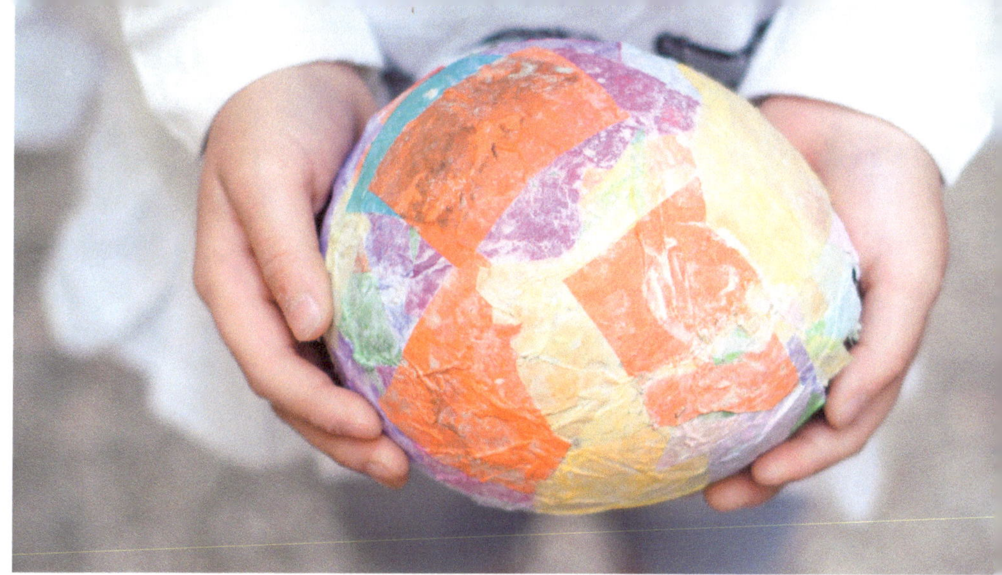

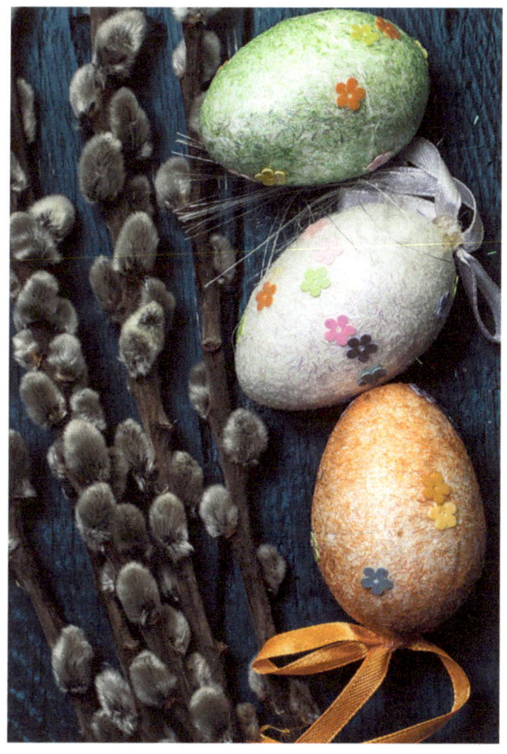

To add even more dimension, glue layers on layers—for example, you might make a green flower with a yellow center or a ladybug sitting atop a leaf.

## Add dimension

If a smooth, uniform egg surface isn't important to you, you can cut small shapes out of thicker paper like cardstock or paper doilies—or even fabric and felt—and glue those on. You're not limited to store-bought stickers!

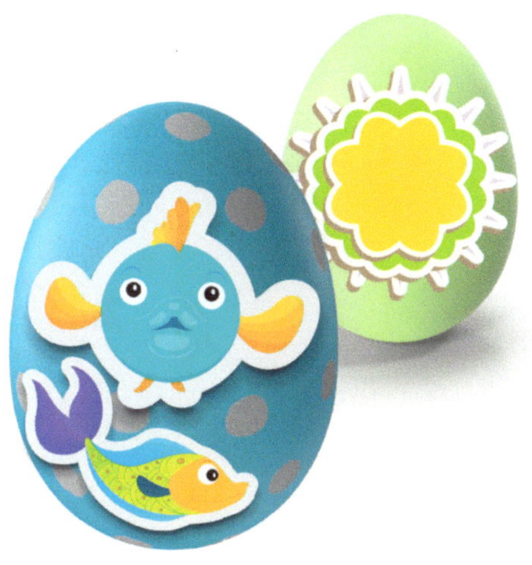

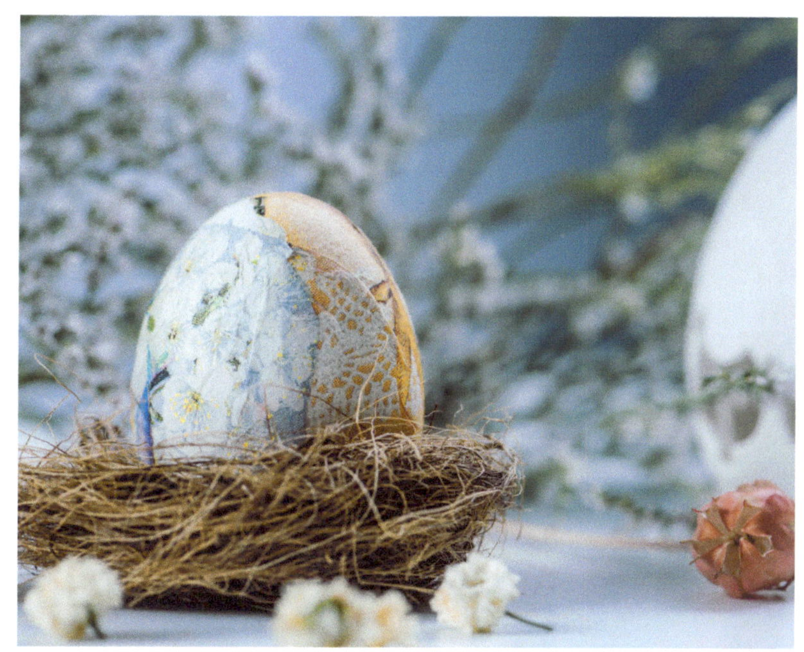

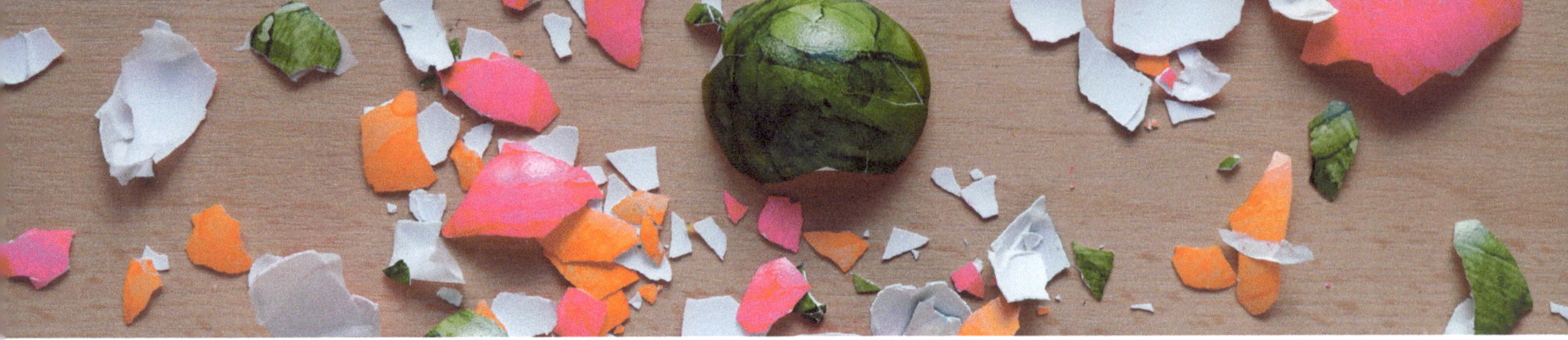

## 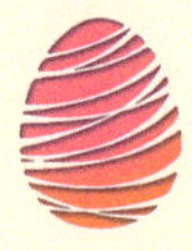 Make mosaic designs with broken eggshells

You can make tile-like mosaic designs on your eggs by breaking colored or uncolored eggshells into small pieces and then layering them over an unbroken egg with decoupage glue.

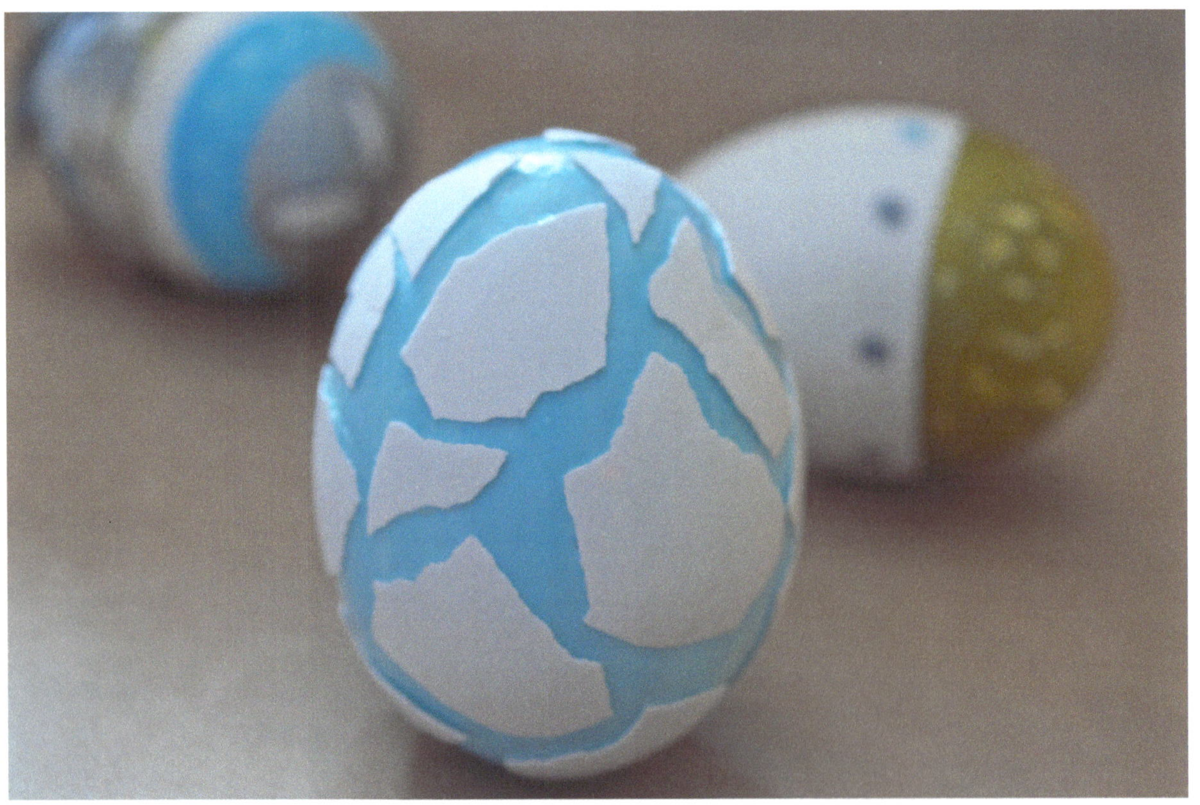

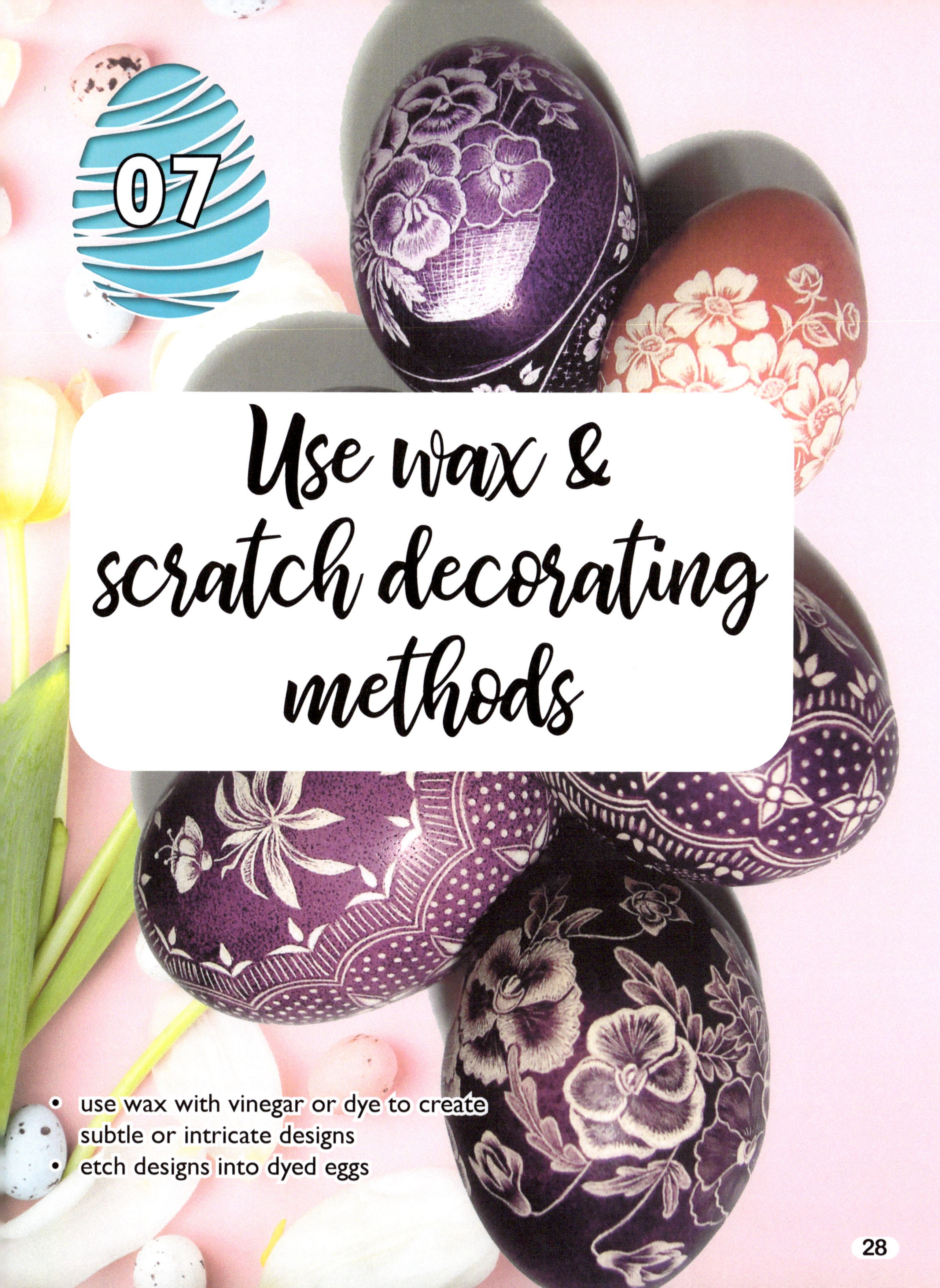


# Use wax & scratch decorating methods

- use wax with vinegar or dye to create subtle or intricate designs
- etch designs into dyed eggs

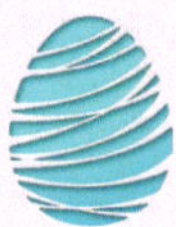

**A**common technique in egg design relies on the fact that wax repels paints, dyes, and vinegar. By applying melted wax to your egg, you create designs that use the negative space left behind on the shell by the wax. Use a combination of vinegar and wax to etch a monochromatic design, or use dye and wax to create a batik-style egg.

Finally, you can also scratch designs onto an eggshell after it's already been colored to achieve results similar to the wax-and-dye method.

## Use wax and vinegar to etch a monochromatic design

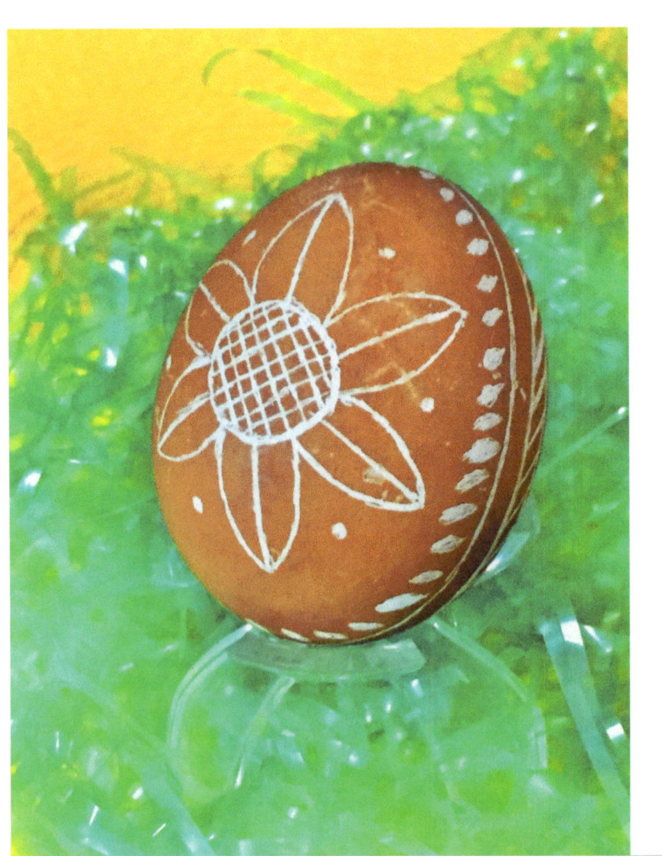

No dyes or paints are needed in this method. Because vinegar has a bleaching and etching effect, the original eggshell color will be the darkest shade in the finished egg. For this reason, it's usually best to use a brown egg. Your design, traced onto the egg in wax, will be the original color of the egg, while the rest of the egg will lighten during the process. How light the egg becomes depends on how long you immerse the egg in vinegar.

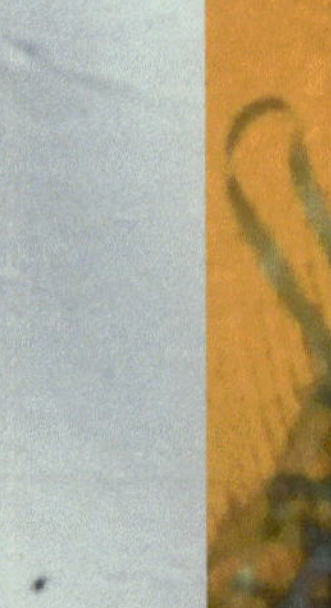

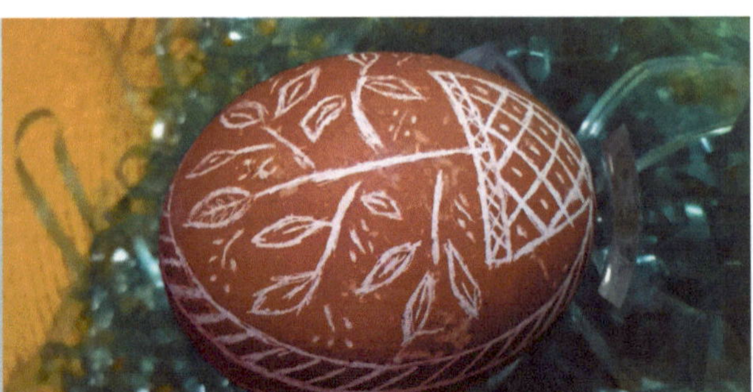

**1** Paint your design on in wax using one of the following two methods:

**For simple designs:** Hold the tip of a crayon or birthday candle over a heat source, such as a tea candle, until it softens enough that you can "paint" your design onto the surface of the egg. Reapply heat, as needed, until you complete your design.

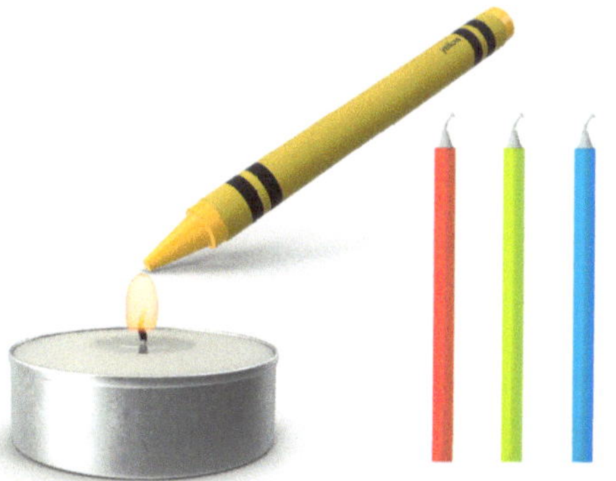

**For more complex designs:** A specialized instrument used in batik called a tjanting (sometimes spelled canting) can be used to create very detailed designs. A tjanting has a reservoir into which melted beeswax is poured. After you add the wax, tip the tjanting forward to start the flow; tilt it backward to stop the flow. Continue filling and applying step by step until your design is completed.

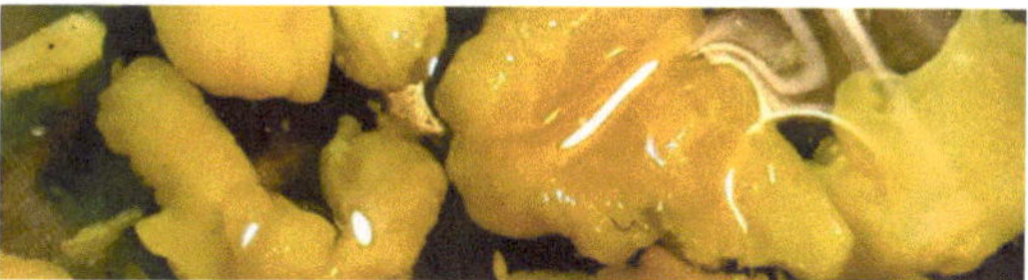

**2** While wearing gloves, place the egg into a cup of vinegar large enough to fully submerge it for 15 minutes to up to 2 hours. The longer the egg is submerged, the lighter the un-waxed color will be and the deeper the engraving. Turn the egg occasionally with a slotted spoon to ensure even coloring.

**3** Remove the egg with a slotted spoon, rinse under water, and allow to dry.

**4** If you would like to add another layer of design, leave the existing wax in place and repeat steps 1-3 as many times as you like. Remember that no bleaching or etching will occur where there is wax.

**5** When you have added all the layers you want and the egg has been rinsed and dried, remove the wax by holding the egg carefully up to a heat source such as a tea candle or hair dryer. Wipe the softened wax away with a cloth. Continue heating and wiping until the egg is free from wax. It will still have a slight sheen from the wax, which is normal.

 # Use wax and dye to create a more colorful design

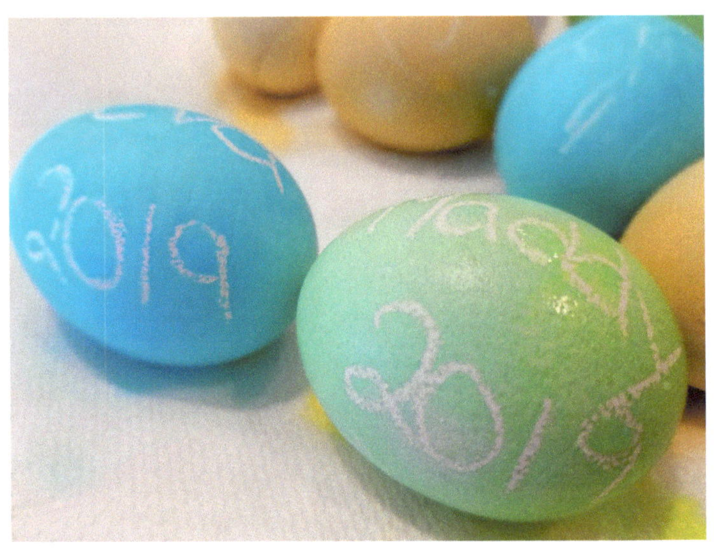

This method is the same as the wax-and-vinegar technique (above), except that a dye, rather than vinegar, is used to create different gradations of color.

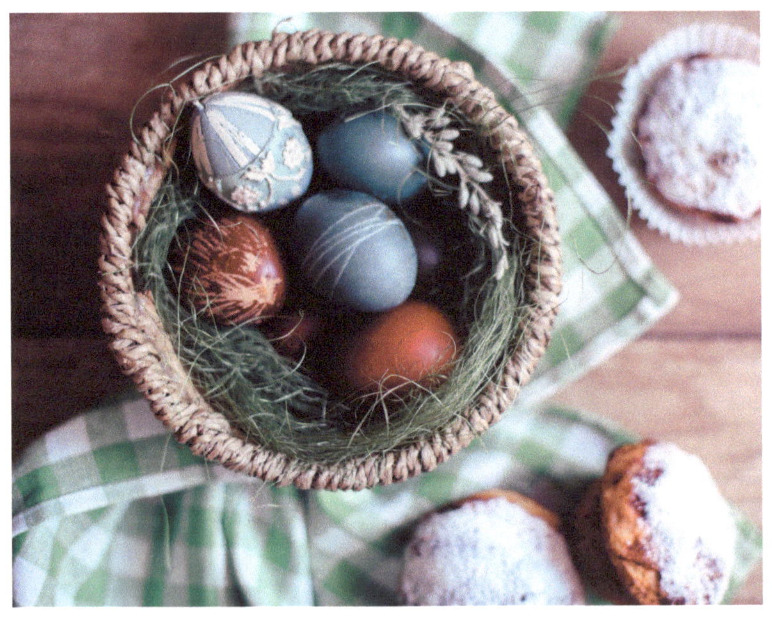

Rather than submerging your egg in vinegar in step 2 (above), submerge it in a cold cup of dye.

If you're feeling very ambitious, you can use more than one layer of wax and color of dye to create a multicolor egg!

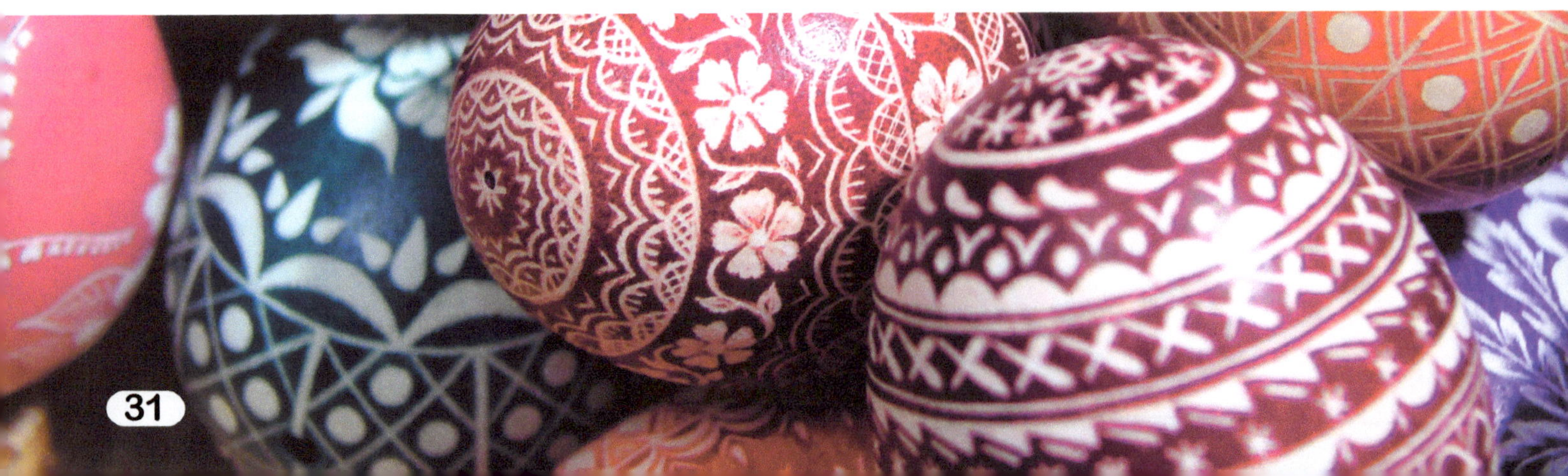

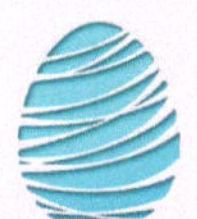 # Scratch designs into dyed eggs

If you like the etched look of vinegar-and-wax eggs but prefer a different approach, with a steady hand you can scratch designs into an eggshell that's already been dyed.

Specialized implements like an awl, engraving tool, or rotary tool equipped with an engraving bit can be used, or you can employ common household items like a needle, razor blade, dental pick, or nail. Whatever tool you choose, use it (carefully!) to scratch a design into the surface of the egg and remove the dye to reveal the original egg color beneath.

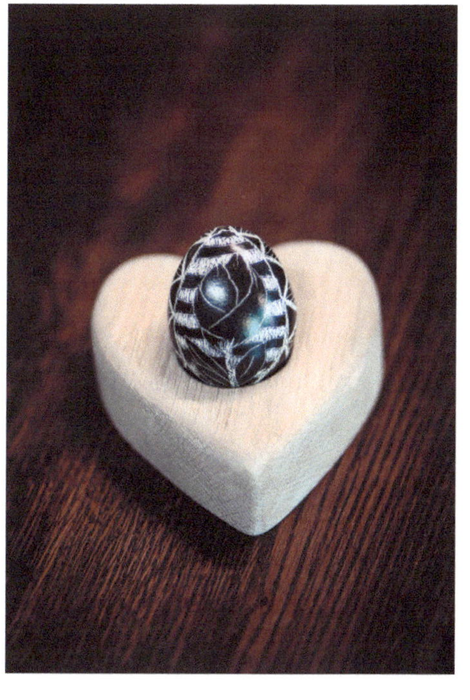

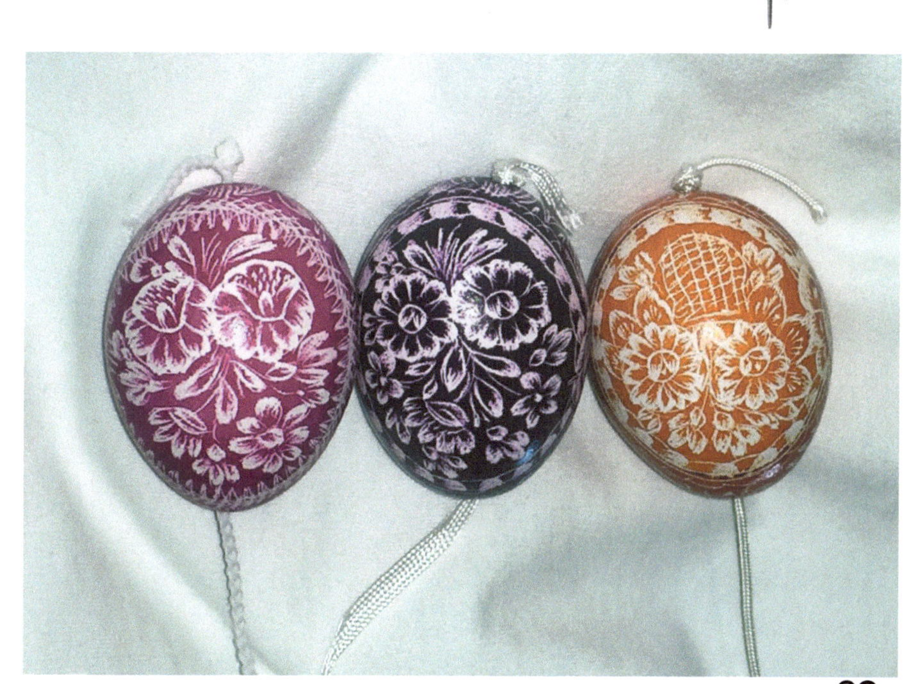

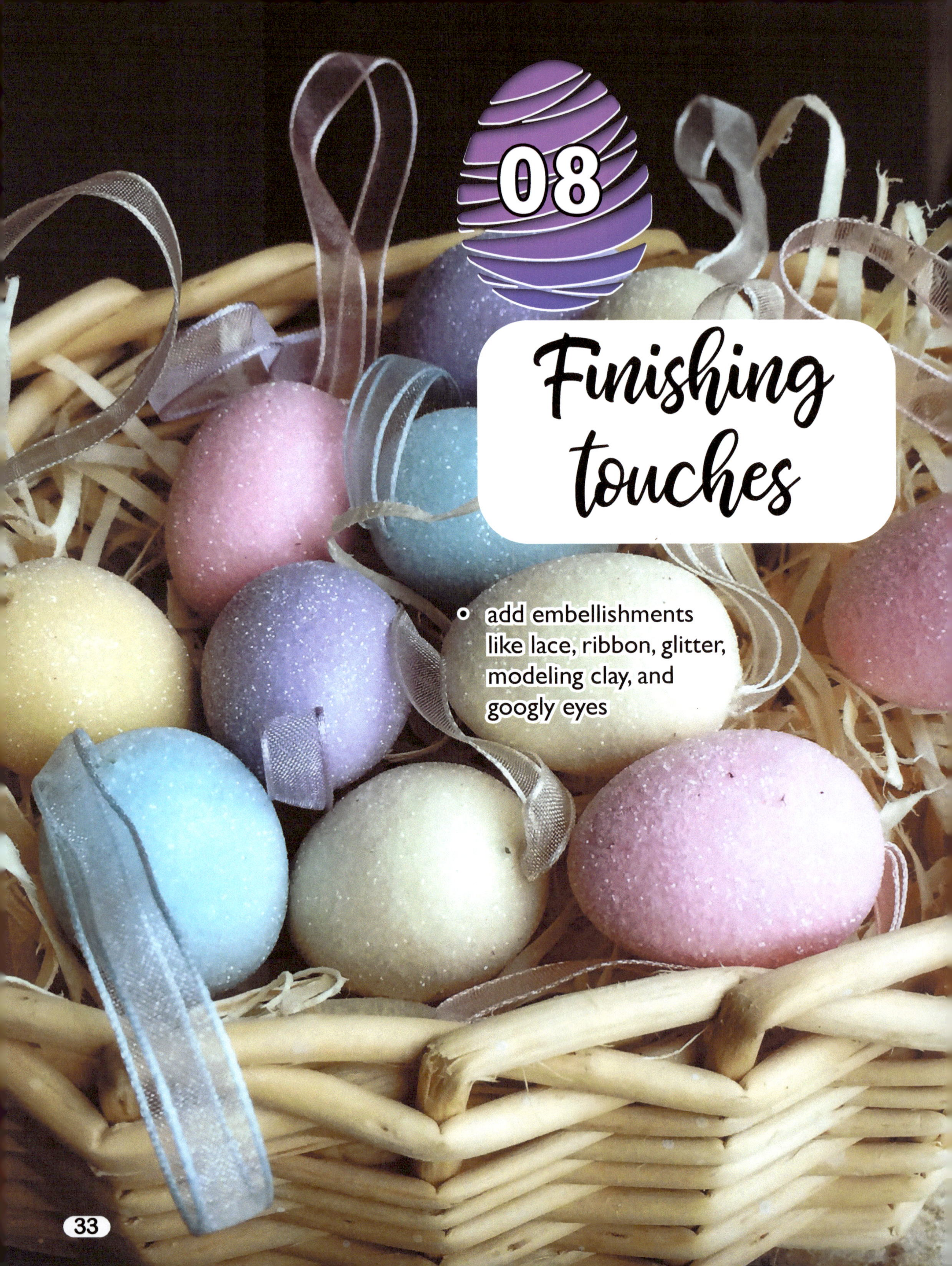

08
Finishing touches

add embellishments
like lace, ribbon, glitter,
modeling clay, and
googly eyes

If you want to jazz up your gorgeous decorated eggs, use decoupage glue or craft glue to add glitter, googly eyes, ribbon, modeling clay, straw—all sorts of things! Make eggs with faces, chicks, bunnies, even people.

Let your imagination run wild as you look at this showcase for inspiration.

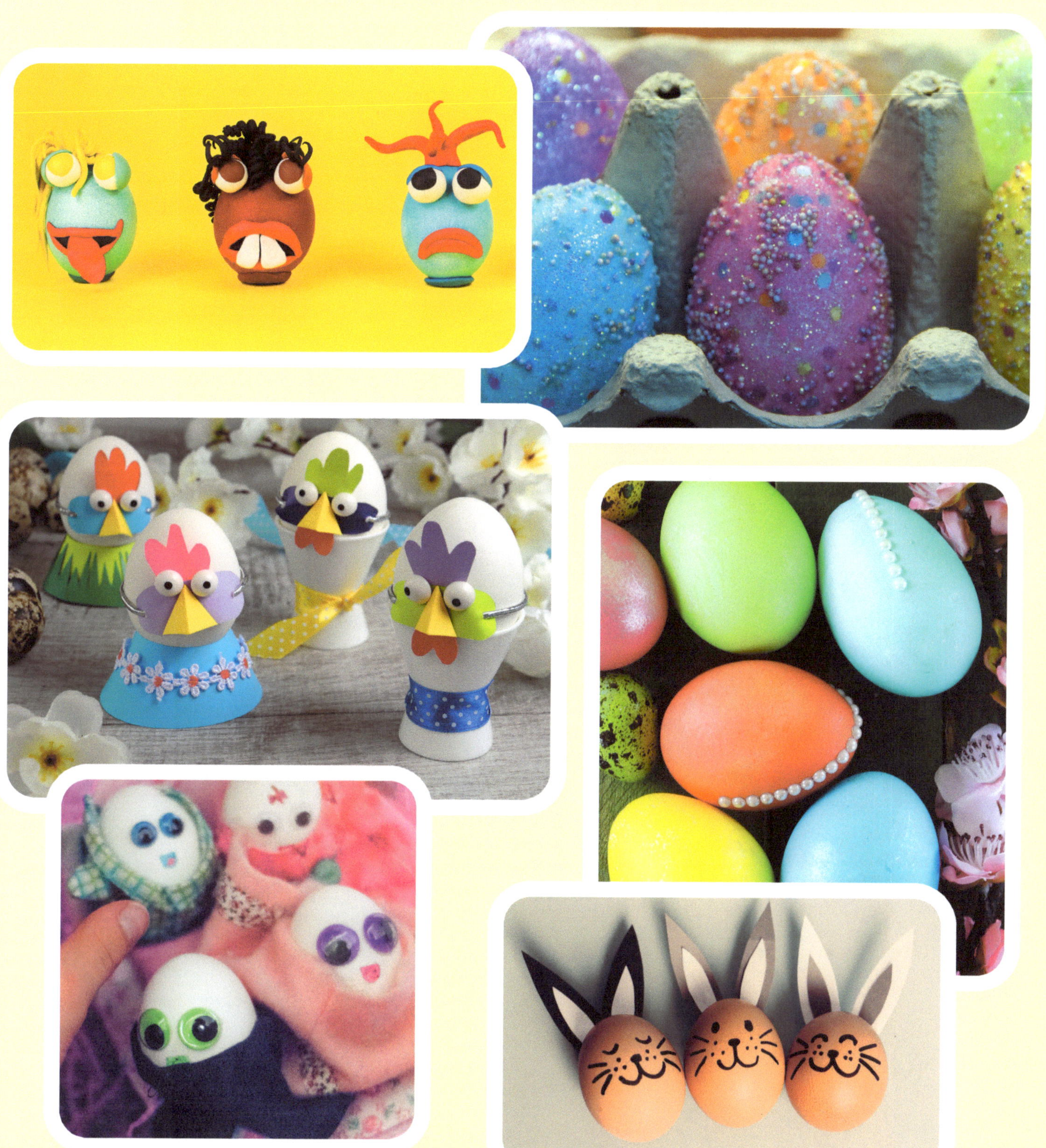

34